Family Favorites:

Tried-and-True Comfort Foods

By

Maureen K. Hurlbut

THE DICTIONARY OF COOKERY.

ALMONDCAKE.

Ingredients.—½ lb. of sweet almonds, 1 oz. of bitter almonds, 6 eggs, 8 tablespoonfuls of sifted sugar, 5 tablespoonfuls of fine flour, the grated rind of 1 lemon, 3 oz. of butter. *Mode.*—Blanch and pound the almonds to a paste; separate the whites from the yolks of the eggs; beat the latter, and add them to the almonds. Stir in the sugar, flour, and lemon-rind; add the butter, which should be beaten to a cream; and, when all these ingredients are well mixed, put in the whites of the eggs, which should be whisked to a stiff froth. Butter a cake-mould, put in the mixture, and bake in a good oven from 1¼ to 1¾ hour. *Time.*—1¼ to 1¾ hour. *Average cost,* 2s. 6d. *Seasonable* at any time.

ALMONDCHEESECAKES.

Ingredients.—¼ lb. of sweet almonds, 4 bitter ones, 3 eggs, 2 oz. of butter, the rind of ¼ lemon, 1 tablespoonful of lemon-juice, 3 oz. of sugar. *Mode.*—Blanch and pound the almonds smoothly in a mortar, with a little rose or spring water; stir in the eggs, which should be well beaten, and the butter, which should be warmed; add the grated lemon-peel and juice, sweeten, and stir well until the whole is thoroughly mixed. Line some patty-pans with puff-paste, put in the mixture, and bake for 20 minutes, or rather less, in a quick oven. *Time.*—20 minutes, or rather less. *Average cost*, 10d. *Sufficient* for about 12 cheesecakes.

ALMONDP ASTE,forSecond-CourseDishes.

Ingredients.—1 lb. of sweet almonds, 6 bitter ones, 1 lb. of very finely-sifted sugar, the whites of 2 eggs. *Mode.*—Blanch the almonds, and dry them thoroughly; put them into a mortar, and pound them well, wetting them gradually with the whites of 2 eggs. When well pounded, put them into a small preserving-pan, add the sugar, and place the pan on a small but clear fire (a hot plate is better); keep stirring until the paste is dry, then take it out of the pan, put it between two dishes, and, when cold, make it into any shape that fancy may dictate. *Time.*—½ hour. *Average cost*, 2s. 8d. for the above quantity. *Sufficient* for 3 small dishes of pastry. *Seasonable* at any time.

ALMOND PUDDING, Baked (very rich).

Ingredients.—¼ lb. of almonds, 4 bitter ditto, 1 glass of sherry, 4 eggs, the rind and juice of ½ lemon, 3 oz. of butter, 1 pint of cream, 2 tablespoonfuls of sugar. *Mode.*—Blanch and pound the almonds to a smooth paste with the water; mix these with the butter, which should be melted; beat up the eggs, grate the lemon-rind, and strain the juice; add these, with the cream, sugar, and wine, to the other ingredients, and stir them well together. When well mixed, put it into a pie-dish lined with puff-paste, and bake for ½ hour. To make this pudding more economically, substitute milk for the cream; but then add rather more than 1 oz. of finely-grated bread. *Time.*—½ to ¾ hour. *Average cost*, 3s., with cream at 1s. 6d. per pint. *Sufficient* for 4 or 5 persons. *Seasonable* at any time.

ALMOND PUDDINGS, Small.

Ingredients.—½ lb. of sweet almonds, 6 bitter ones, ¼ lb. of butter, 4 eggs, 2 tablespoonfuls of sifted sugar, 2 tablespoonfuls of cream, 1 tablespoonful of brandy. *Mode.*—Blanch and pound the almonds to a smooth paste with a spoonful of water; warm the butter, mix the almonds with this, and add the other ingredients, leaving out the whites of 2 eggs, and be particular that these are well beaten. Mix well, butter some cups, half fill them, and bake the puddings from 20 minutes to ½ hour. Turn them out on a dish, and serve with sweet sauce, or with sifted sugar only. *Time.*—20 minutes to ½ hour. *Average cost*, 2s. *Sufficient* for 4 or 5 persons. *Seasonable* at any time.

SMALL ALMOND PUDDINGS.

ALMOND PUFFS.

Ingredients.—2 tablespoonfuls of flour, 2 oz. of butter, 2 oz. of pounded sugar, 2 oz. of sweet almonds, 4 bitter almonds. *Mode.*—Blanch and pound the almonds in a mortar to a smooth paste; melt the butter, dredge in the flour, and add the sugar and pounded almonds. Beat the mixture well, and put it into cups or very tiny jelly-pots, which should be well buttered, and bake in a moderate oven for about 20 minutes, or longer, should the puffs be large. Turn them out on a dish, the bottom of the puff uppermost, and serve. *Time.*—20 minutes. *Average cost*, 8*d*. *Sufficient* for 2 or 3 persons. *Seasonable* at any time.

ALMONDSOUP.

Ingredients.—4 lbs. of lean beef or veal, a few vegetables as for Stock (*see* Stock), 1 oz. of vermicelli, 4 blades of mace, 6 cloves, ½ lb. of sweet almonds, the yolks of 6 eggs, 1 gill of thick cream, rather more than 3 quarts of water. *Mode.*—Boil the beef or veal, vegetables, and spices gently in water that will cover them, till the gravy is very strong, and the meat very tender; than strain off the gravy, and set it on the fire with the specified quantity of vermicelli to 2 quarts. Let it boil till sufficiently cooked. Have ready the almonds, blanched and pounded very fine; the yolks of the eggs boiled hard; mixing the almonds, whilst pounding, with a little of the soup, lest the latter should grow oily. Pound them to a pulp, and keep adding to them, by degrees, a little soup, until they are thoroughly mixed together. Let the soup be cool when mixing, and do it perfectly smooth. Strain it through a sieve, set it on the fire, stir frequently, and serve hot. Just before taking it up, add the cream. *Time.*—From 4 to 5 hours to simmer meat and vegetables; 20 minutes to cook the vermicelli. *Average cost* per quart, 2*s*. 3*d*. *Seasonable* all the year. *Sufficient* for 8 persons.

ANCHOVYBUTTER.

Ingredients.—To every lb. of butter allow 6 anchovies, 1 small bunch of parsley. *Mode.*—Wash, bone, and pound the anchovies well in a mortar; scald the parsley, chop it, and rub through a sieve; then pound all the ingredients together, mix well, and make the butter into pats immediately. This makes a pretty dish, if fancifully moulded, for breakfast or supper, and should be garnished with parsley. *Average cost*, 1s. 8d. *Sufficient* to make 2 dishes, with 4 small pats each. *Seasonable* at any time.

ANCHOVY SAUCE, for Fish.

Ingredients.—4 anchovies, 1 oz. of butter, ½ pint of melted butter, cayenne to taste. *Mode.*—Bone the anchovies, and pound them in a mortar to a paste, with 1 oz. of butter. Make the melted butter hot, stir in the pounded anchovies and cayenne; simmer for 3 or 4 minutes; and, if liked, add a squeeze of lemon-juice. A more general and expeditious way of making this sauce is to stir in 1½ tablespoonfuls of anchovy essence to ½ pint of melted butter, and to add seasoning to taste. Boil the whole up for 1 minute, and serve hot. *Time.*—5 minutes. *Average cost*, 6d. for ½ pint. *Sufficient*, this quantity, for a brill, small turbot, 2 soles, &c.

ANCHOVY TOAST.

Ingredients.—Toast 2 or 3 slices of bread, or, if wanted very savoury, fry them in clarified butter, and spread on them the paste made by recipe for potted anchovies. Made mustard, or a few grains of cayenne, may be added to the paste before laying it on the toast.

ANCHOVIES, Fried.

Ingredients.—1 tablespoonful of oil, ½ a glass of white wine, sufficient flour to thicken; 12 anchovies. *Mode.*—Mix the oil and wine together, with sufficient flour to make them into a thickish paste; cleanse the anchovies, wipe them, dip them in the paste, and fry of a nice brown colour. *Time.*—½ hour. *Average cost*, for this quantity, 9d. *Sufficient* for 2 persons. *Seasonable* all the year.

ANCHOVIES, Potted, or Anchovy Butter.

Ingredients.—2 dozen anchovies, ½ lb. of fresh butter. *Mode.*—Wash the anchovies thoroughly; bone and dry them, and pound them in a mortar to a paste. Mix the butter gradually with them, and rub the whole through a sieve. Put it by in small pots for use, and carefully exclude the air with a bladder, as it soon changes the colour of anchovies, besides spoiling them.

To potted anchovies may be added pounded mace, cayenne, and nutmeg to taste.

APPLE CHARLOTTE, a very simple.

Ingredients.—9 slices of bread and butter, about 6 good-sized apples, 1 tablespoonful of minced lemon-peel, 2 tablespoonfuls of juice, moist sugar to taste. *Mode.*—Butter a pie-dish; place a layer of bread and butter, without the crust, at the bottom; then a layer of apples, pared, cored, and cut into thin slices; sprinkle over these a portion of the lemon-peel and juice, and sweeten with moist sugar. Place another layer of bread and butter, and then one of apples, proceeding in this manner until the dish is full; then cover it up with the peel of the apples, to preserve the top from browning or burning; bake in a brisk oven for rather more than ¾ hour; turn the charlotte on a dish, sprinkle sifted sugar over, and serve. *Time.*—¾ hour, or a few minutes longer. *Average cost*, 1s. *Sufficient* for 5 or 6 persons. *Seasonable* from August to March.

APPLE CHEESECAKES.

Ingredients.—½ lb. of apple pulp, ¼ lb. of sifted sugar, ¼ lb. of butter, 4 eggs, the rind and juice of 1 lemon. *Mode.*—Pare, core, and boil sufficient apples to make ½ lb. when cooked; add to these the sugar, the butter, which should be melted, the eggs, leaving out 2 of the whites, and the grated rind and juice of 1 lemon; stir the mixture well; line some patty-pans with puff-paste; put in the mixture, and bake about 20 minutes.—*Time.*—About 20 minutes. *Average cost*, for the above quantity, with the paste, 1s. 6d. *Sufficient* for about 18 or 20 cheesecakes. *Seasonable* from August to March.

APPLE CUSTARD, Baked.

Ingredients.—1 dozen large apples, moist sugar to taste, 1 small teacupful of cold water, the grated rind of 1 lemon, 1 pint of milk, 4 eggs, 2 oz. of loaf sugar. *Mode.*—Peel, cut, and core the apples; put them into a lined saucepan with the cold water, and, as they heat, bruise them to a pulp; sweeten with moist sugar, and add the grated lemon-rind. When cold, put the fruit at the bottom of a pie-dish, and pour over it a custard, made with the above proportion of milk, eggs, and sugar; grate a little nutmeg over the top, place the dish in a moderate oven, and bake from 25 to 35 minutes. The above proportions will make rather a large dish. *Time.*—25 to 35 minutes. *Averagecost*, 1*s.* 6*d.*, if fruit has to be bought. *Sufficient* for 6 or 7 persons. *Seasonable* from August to March.

APPLEDUMPLINGS,Baked(PlainfamilyDish).

Ingredients.—6 apples, suet-crust, sugar to taste. *Mode.*—Pare and take out the cores of the apples with a scoop, and make a suet-crust with ¾ lb. of flour to 6 oz. of suet; roll the apples in the crust, previously sweetening them with moist sugar, and taking care to join the paste nicely. When they are formed into round balls, put them on a tin, and bake them for about ½ hour, or longer, should the apples be very large; arrange them pyramidically on a dish, and sift over them some pounded white sugar. These may be made richer by using puff-paste instead of suet-crust. *Time.*—From ½ to ¾ hour, or longer. *Average cost*, 1½*d.* each. *Sufficient* for 4 persons. *Seasonable* from August to March, but flavourless after the end of January.

APPLEDUMPLINGS,Boiled.

Ingredients.—6 apples, suet-crust, sugar to taste. *Mode.*—Pare and take out the cores of the apples with a scoop; sweeten, and roll each apple in a piece of crust, made with ¾ lb. of flour to 6 oz. of suet, and be particular that the paste is nicely joined. Put the dumplings into floured cloths, tie them securely, and place them in boiling water. Keep them boiling from ¾ to 1 hour; remove the cloths, and send them hot and quickly to table. Dumplings boiled in knitted cloths have a very pretty appearance when they come to table. The cloths should be made square, just large enough to hold one dumpling, and should be knitted in plain knitting, with *very coarse* cotton. *Time.*—¾ to 1 hour, or longer should the dumplings be very large. *Average cost*, 1½*d.* each. *Sufficient* for 4 persons. *Seasonable* from August to March, but flavourless after the end of January.

APPLEFRITTERS.

Ingredients.—For the batter, 2 tablespoonfuls of flour, ½ oz. of butter, ½ saltspoonful of salt, 2 eggs, milk, 4 medium-sized apples, hot lard or clarified beef-dripping. *Mode.*—Break the eggs, dividing the whites from the yolks, and beat them separately. Put the flour into a basin, stir in the butter, which should be melted to a cream; add the salt, and moisten with sufficient warm milk to make it of a proper consistency, that is to say, a batter that will drop from the spoon. Stir this well, rub down any lumps that may be seen, add the yolks and then the whites of the eggs, which have been previously well whisked; beat up the batter for a few minutes, and it is ready for use. Now peel and cut the apples into rather thick whole slices, without dividing them, and stamp out the middle of each slice, where the core is, with a cutter. Throw the slices into the batter; have ready a pan of boiling lard or clarified dripping; take out the pieces of apple one by one, put them into the hot lard, and fry a nice brown, turning them when required. When done, lay them on a piece of blotting-paper before the fire, to absorb the greasy moisture; then dish on a white d'oyley, piling the fritters one above the other; strew over them some pounded sugar, and serve very hot. The flavour of the fritters would be very much improved by soaking the pieces of apple in a little wine, mixed with sugar and lemon-juice, for 3 or 4 hours before wanted for table; the batter, also, is better for being mixed some hours before the fritters are made. *Time.*—From 7 to 10 minutes to fry the fritters; 5 minutes to drain them. *Average cost,* 9d. *Sufficient* for 4 or 5 persons. *Seasonable* from August to March.

APPLEJAM.

Ingredients.—To every lb. of fruit weighed after being pared, cored, and sliced, allow ¾ lb. of preserving-sugar, the grated rind of 1 lemon, the juice of ½ lemon. *Mode.*—Peel the apples, core and slice them very thin, and be particular that they are all the same sort. Put them into a jar, stand this in a saucepan of boiling water, and let the apples stew until quite tender. Previously to putting the fruit into the jar, weigh it, to ascertain the proportion of sugar that may be required. Put the apples into a preserving-pan, crush the sugar to small lumps, and add it, with the grated lemon-rind and juice, to the apples. Simmer these over the fire for ½ hour, reckoning from the time the jam begins to simmer properly; remove the scum as it rises, and, when the jam is done, put it into pots for use. Place a piece of oiled paper over the jam, and, to exclude the air, cover the pots with tissue paper dipped in the white of an egg, and stretched over the top. This jam will keep good for a long time. *Time.*—From 3 to 4 hours to stew in the jar; ½ hour to boil after the jam begins to simmer. *Average cost*, for this quantity, 5*s*. *Sufficient.*—7 or 8 lbs. of apples for 6 pots of jam. *Seasonable.*—Make this in September, October, or November, when apples can be bought at a reasonable price.

APPLEJELL Y.

Ingredients.—To 6 lbs. of apples allow 3 pints of water; to every quart of juice allow 2 lbs. of loaf sugar;—the juice of ½ lemon. *Mode.*—Pare, core, and cut the apples into slices, and put them into a jar, with water in the above proportion. Place them in a cool oven, with the jar well covered, and, when the juice is thoroughly drawn and the apples are quite soft, strain them through a jelly-bag. To every quart of juice allow 2 lbs. of loaf sugar, which should be crushed to small lumps, and put into a preserving-pan with the juice. Boil these together for rather more than ½ hour, remove the scum as it rises, add the lemon-juice just before it is done, and put the jelly into pots for use. This preparation is useful for garnishing sweet dishes, and may be turned out for dessert. *Time.*—The apples to be put in the oven over-night, and left till morning; rather more than ½ hour to boil the jelly. *Average cost*, for this quantity, 3*s*. *Sufficient* for 6 small pots of jelly. *Seasonable.*—This should be made in September, October, or November.

APPLEJELL Y.

Ingredients.—Apples, water; to every pint of syrup allow ¾ lb. of loaf sugar. *Mode.*—Pare and cut the apples into pieces, remove the cores, and put them in a preserving-pan with sufficient cold water to cover them. Let them boil for an hour; then drain the syrup from them through a hair sieve or jelly-bag, and measure the juice; to every pint allow ¾ lb. of loaf sugar, and boil these together for ¾ hour, removing every particle of scum as it rises, and keeping the jelly well stirred, that it may not burn. A little lemon-rind may be boiled with the apples, and a small quantity of strained lemon-juice may be put in the jelly just before it is done, when the flavour is liked. This jelly may be ornamented with preserved greengages, or any other preserved fruit, and will turn out very prettily for dessert. It should be stored away in small pots. *Time.*—1 hour to boil the fruit and water; ¾ hour to boil the juice with the sugar. *Average cost*, for 6 lbs. of apples, with the other ingredients in proportion, 3s. *Sufficient* for 6 small pots of jelly. *Seasonable.*—Make this in September, October, or November.

APPLE JELLY, Clear, for immediate Eating.

Ingredients.—2 dozen small apples, 1½ pint of spring-water; to every pint of juice allow ½ lb. of loaf sugar, ½ oz. of isinglass, the rind of ½ lemon. *Mode.*—Pare, core, and cut the apples into quarters, and boil them, with the lemon-peel, until tender; then strain off the apples, and run the juice through a jelly-bag; put the strained juice, with the sugar and isinglass, which has been previously boiled in ½ pint of water, into a lined saucepan or preserving-pan; boil all together for about ½ hour, and put the jelly into moulds. When this jelly is clear, and turned out well, it makes a pretty addition to the supper-table, with a little custard or whipped cream round it: a little lemon-juice improves the flavour, but it is apt to render the jelly muddy and thick. If required to be kept any length of time, rather a larger proportion of sugar must be used. *Time.*—About 1 hour to boil the apples; ½ hour the jelly. *Average cost*, 2s. *Sufficient* for 1½-pint mould. *Seasonable* from August to March.

APPLE JELLY, Thick, or Marmalade, for Entremets or Dessert Dishes.

Ingredients.—Apples; to every lb. of pulp allow ¾ lb. of sugar, ½ teaspoonful of minced lemon-peel. *Mode.*—Peel, core, and boil the apples with only sufficient water to prevent them from burning; beat them to a pulp, and to every lb. of pulp allow the above proportion of sugar in lumps. Dip the lumps into water; put these into a saucepan, and boil till the syrup is thick and can be well skimmed; then add this syrup to the apple pulp, with the minced lemon-peel, and stir it over a quick fire for about 20 minutes, or till the apples cease to stick to the bottom of the pan. The jelly is then done, and may be poured into moulds which have been previously dipped in water, when it will turn out nicely for dessert or a side dish; for the latter, a little custard should be poured round, and it should be garnished with strips of citron or stuck with blanched almonds. *Time.*—From ½ to ¾ hour to reduce the apples to a pulp; 20 minutes to boil after the sugar is added.

Sufficient.—1½ lb. of apple pulp sufficient for a small mould. *Seasonable* from August to March; but is best and cheapest in September, October, or November.

APPLE JELLY, STUCK WITH ALMONDS.

APPLE PUDDING, Rich Baked.

Ingredients.—½ lb. apple pulp, ½ lb. of loaf sugar, 6 oz. of butter, the rind of 1 lemon, 6 eggs, puff-paste. *Mode.*—Peel, core, and cut the apples, as for sauce; put them into a stewpan, with only just sufficient water to prevent them from burning, and let them stew until reduced to a pulp. Weigh the pulp, and to every ½ lb. add the sifted sugar, grated lemon-rind, and 6 well-beaten eggs. Beat these ingredients well together; then melt the butter, stir it to the other things, put a border of puff-paste round the dish, and bake for rather more than ½ hour. The butter should not be added until the pudding is ready for the oven. *Time.*—½ to ¾ hour. *Average cost*, 1s. 10d. *Sufficient* for 5 or 6 persons. *Seasonable* from August to March.

APPLE PUDDING, Baked.

Ingredients.—12 large apples, 6 oz. of moist sugar, ¼ lb. of butter, 4 eggs, 1 pint of bread-crumbs. *Mode.*—Pare, core, and cut the apples, as for sauce, and boil them until reduced to a pulp; then add the butter, melted, and the eggs, which should be well whisked. Beat up the pudding for 2 or 3 minutes; butter a pie-dish; put in a layer of bread-crumbs, then the apple, and then another layer of bread-crumbs; flake over these a few tiny pieces of butter, and bake for about ½ hour. A very good economical pudding may be made merely with apples, boiled and sweetened, with the addition of a few strips of lemon-peel. A layer of bread-crumbs should be placed above and below the apples, and the pudding baked for ½ hour. *Time.*—About ½ hour. *Average cost,* 1*s.* 6*d. Sufficient* for 5 or 6 persons. *Seasonable* from August to March.

APPLE PUDDING, Baked (Very Good).

Ingredients.—5 moderate-sized apples, 2 tablespoonfuls of finely-chopped suet, 3 eggs, 3 tablespoonfuls of flour, 1 pint of milk, a little grated nutmeg. *Mode.*—Mix the flour to a smooth batter with the milk, add the eggs, which should be well whisked, and put the latter into a well-buttered pie-dish. Wipe the apples clean, but do not pare them; cut them in halves, and take out the cores; lay them in the batter, rind uppermost; shake the suet on the top, over which also grate a little nutmeg; bake in a moderate oven for an hour, and cover, when served, with sifted loaf sugar. This pudding is also very good with the apples pared, sliced, and mixed with the batter. *Time.*—1 hour. *Average cost*, 9*d. Sufficient* for 5 or 6 persons.

APPLE PUDDING, Boiled.

Ingredients.—Suet crust, apples, sugar to taste, 1 small teaspoonful of finely-minced lemon-peel, 2 tablespoonfuls of lemon-juice. *Mode.*—Make a butter or suet crust by either of the given recipes, using for a moderate-sized pudding from ¾ to 1 lb. of flour, with the other ingredients in proportion. Butter a basin; line it with some paste; pare, core, and cut the apples into slices, and fill the basin with these; add the sugar, the lemon-peel and juice; and cover with crust; pinch the edges together, flour the cloth, place it over the pudding, tie it securely, and put it into plenty of fast-boiling water; let it boil from 2½ to 3 hours; then turn it out of the basin and send to table quickly. Apple puddings may also be boiled in a cloth without a basin; but, when made in this way, must be served without the least delay, as the crust soon becomes heavy. Apple pudding is a very convenient dish to have when the dinner-hour is rather uncertain, as it does not spoil by being boiled an extra hour; care, however, must be taken to keep it well covered with water all the time, and not to allow it to stop boiling. *Time.*—From 2½ to 3 hours, according to the quality of the apples. *Average* cost, 10*d. Sufficient*, made with 1 lb. of flour, for 7 or 8 persons. *Seasonable* from August to March; but the apples become flavourless and scarce after February.

APPLE SAUCE, for Geese, Pork, &c.

Ingredients.—6 good-sized apples, sifted sugar to taste, a piece of butter the size of a walnut; water. *Mode.*—Pare, core, and quarter the apples, and throw them into cold water to preserve their whiteness. Put them in a saucepan, with sufficient water to moisten them, and boil till soft enough to pulp. Beat them up, adding sugar to taste, and a small piece of butter. This quantity is sufficient for a good-sized tureen. *Time.*—According to the apples, about, ¾ hour. *Average cost*, 4d. *Sufficient*, this quantity, for a goose or couple of ducks.

APPLE SNOW (a pretty Supper Dish).

Ingredients.—10 good-sized apples, the whites of 10 eggs, the rind of 1 lemon, ½ lb. of pounded sugar. *Mode.*—Peel, core, and cut the apples into quarters, and put them into a saucepan with the lemon-peel, and sufficient water to prevent them from burning,—rather less than ½ pint. When they are tender, take out the peel, beat them into a pulp, let them cool, and stir them to the whites of the eggs, which should be previously beaten to a strong froth. Add the sifted sugar, and continue the whisking until the mixture becomes quite stiff, and either heap it on a glass dish or serve it in small glasses. The dish may be garnished with preserved barberries or strips of bright-coloured jelly, and a dish of custards should be served with it, or a jug of cream. *Time.*—From 30 to 40 minutes to stew the apples. *Average cost*, 1s. 6d. *Sufficient* to fill a moderate-sized glass dish. *Seasonable* from August to March.

APPLE SNOWBALLS.

Ingredients.—2 teacupfuls of rice, apples, moist sugar, cloves. *Mode.*—Boil the rice and milk until three-parts done; then strain it off, and pare and core the apples without dividing them. Put a small quantity of sugar and a clove into each apple, put the rice round them, and tie each ball separately in a cloth. Boil until the apples are tender; then take them up, remove the cloths, and serve. *Time.*—½ hour to boil the rice separately; ½ to 1 hour with the apple. *Seasonable* from August to March.

APPLE SOUFFLÉ.

Ingredients.—6 oz. of rice, 1 quart of milk, the rind of ½ lemon, sugar to taste, the yolks of 4 eggs, the whites of 6, 1½ oz. of butter, 4 tablespoonfuls of apple marmalade. *Mode.*—Boil the milk with the lemon-peel until the former is well flavoured; then strain it, put in the rice, and let it gradually swell over a slow fire, adding sufficient sugar to sweeten it nicely. Then crush the rice to a smooth pulp with the back of a wooden spoon; line the bottom and sides of a round cake-tin with it, and put it into the oven to set; turn it out of the tin dexterously, and be careful that the border of rice is firm in every part. Mix with the marmalade the beaten yolks of eggs and the butter, and stir these over the fire until the mixture thickens. Take it off the fire; to this add the whites of the eggs, which should be previously beaten to a strong froth; stir all together, and put it into the rice border. Bake in a moderate oven for about ½ hour, or until the soufflé rises very light. It should be watched, and served instantly, or it will immediately fall after it is taken from the oven. *Time.*—½ hour. *Average cost*, 1*s.* 8*d.* *Sufficient* for 4 or 5 persons. *Seasonable* from August to March.

APPLE TART or PIE.

Ingredients.—Puff-paste, apples; to every lb. of unpared apples allow 2 oz. of moist sugar, ½ teaspoonful of finely-minced lemon-peel, 1 tablespoonful of lemon-juice. *Mode.*—Make puff-paste by either of the given recipes, with ½ lb. of flour; place a border of it round the edge of a pie-dish, and fill the dish with apples pared, cored, and cut into slices; sweeten with moist sugar, add the lemon-peel and juice, and 2 or 3 tablespoonfuls of water; cover with crust, cut it evenly round close to the edge of the pie-dish, and bake in a hot oven from ½ to ¾ hour, or rather longer, should the pie be very large. When it is three-parts done, take it out of the oven, put the white of an egg on a plate, and, with the blade of a knife, whisk it to a froth; brush the pie over with this, then sprinkle upon it some sifted sugar, and then a few drops of water. Put the pie back into the oven, and finish baking, and be particularly careful that it does not catch or burn, *whichitisveryliabletodoafterthecrustisiced* . If made with a plain crust, the icing may be omitted. Many things are suggested for the flavouring of apple pie; some say 2 or 3 tablespoonfuls of beer, others the same quantity of sherry, which very much improve the taste; whilst the old-fashioned addition of a few cloves is, by many persons, preferred to anything else, as also a few slices of quince. *Time.*—½ hour before the crust is iced; 10 to 15 minutes afterwards. *Averagecost*, 9d. *Sufficient.*—Allow 2 lbs. of apples to a tart for 6 persons. *Seasonable* from August to March; but the apples become flavourless after February.

APPLE TART (Creamed).

Mode.—Make an apple tart by the preceding recipe, with the exception of omitting the icing. When the tart is baked, cut out the middle of the lid or crust, leaving a border all round the dish. Fill up with a nicely-made boiled custard, grate a little nutmeg over the top, and the pie is ready for table. This tart is usually eaten cold; is rather an old-fashioned dish, but, at the same time, extremely nice. *Time.*—½ to ¾ hour. *Average cost*, 1s. 3d. *Sufficient* for 5 or 6 persons. *Seasonable* from August to March.

APPLE TRIFLE (a Supper Dish).

Ingredients.—10 good-sized apples, the rind of ½ lemon, 6 oz. of pounded sugar, ½ pint of milk, ½ pint of cream, 2 eggs, whipped cream. *Mode.*—Peel, core, and cut the apples into thin slices, and put them into a saucepan with 2 tablespoonfuls of water, the sugar, and minced lemon-rind. Boil all together until quite tender, and pulp the apples through a sieve; if they should not be quite sweet enough, add a little more sugar, and put them at the bottom of the dish to form a thick layer. Stir together the milk, cream, and eggs, with a little sugar, over the fire, and let the mixture thicken, but do not allow it to reach the boiling-point. When thick, take it off the fire; let it cool a little, then pour it over the apples. Whip some cream with sugar, lemon-peel, &c., the same as for other trifles; heap it high over the custard, and the dish is ready for table. It may be garnished as fancy dictates, with strips of bright apple jelly, slices of citron, &c. *Time.*—From 30 to 40 minutes to stew the apples; 10 minutes to stir the custard over the fire. *Average cost*, 2s., with cream at 1s. 6d. per pint. *Sufficient* for a moderate-sized trifle. *Seasonable* from August to March.

APPLES à la Portugaise.

Ingredients.—8 good boiling apples, ½ pint of water, 6 oz. of sugar, a layer of apple marmalade, 8 preserved cherries, garnishing of apricot jam. *Mode.*—Peel the apples, and, with a scoop, take out the cores; boil the fruit in the above proportion of sugar and water, without being too much done, and take care the apples do not break. Have ready some apple marmalade; cover the bottom of a glass dish with this, level it, and lay the apples in a sieve to drain; pile them neatly on the marmalade, raising them in the centre, and place a preserved cherry in the middle of each. Garnish with strips of candied citron or apricot jam, and the dish is ready for table. *Time.*—From 20 to 30 minutes to stew the apples. *Averagecost*, 1s. 3d. *Sufficient* for 1 entremets. *Seasonable* from August to March.

APPLES,Butter ed(SweetEntr emets).

Ingredients.—Apple marmalade or 7 good boiling apples, ½ pint of water, 6 oz. of sugar, 2 oz. of butter, a little apricot jam. *Mode.*—Pare the apples, and take out the cores with a scoop; boil up the sugar and water for a few minutes; then lay in the apples and simmer them very gently until tender, taking care not to let them break. Have ready sufficient marmalade made by the recipe for <u>Apple Marmalade</u>, flavoured with lemon, to cover the bottom of the dish; arrange the apples on this with a piece of butter placed in each, and in between them a few spoonfuls of apricot jam or marmalade; put the dish in the oven for 10 minutes, then sprinkle over the top sifted sugar, and either brown it before the fire or with a salamander, and serve hot. The syrup that the apples were boiled in should be saved for another time. *Time.*—From 20 to 30 minutes to stew the apples very gently, 10 minutes in the oven. *Averagecost*, 1s. 6d. *Sufficient* for 1 entremets.

APPLESandRICE(aPlainDish).

Ingredients.—8 good-sized apples, 3 oz. of butter, the rind of ½ lemon minced very fine, 6 oz. of rice, 1½ pints of milk, sugar to taste, ½ teaspoonful of grated nutmeg, 6 tablespoonfuls of apricot jam. *Mode.*—Peel the apples, halve them, and take out the cores; put them into a stewpan with the butter, and strew sufficient sifted sugar over to sweeten them nicely, and add the minced lemon-peel. Stew the apples very gently until tender, taking care they do not break. Boil the rice, with the milk, sugar, and nutmeg, until soft, and, when thoroughly done, dish it, piled high in the centre; arrange the apples on it, warm the apricot jam, pour it over the whole, and serve hot. *Time.*—About 30 minutes to stew the apples very gently; about ¾ hour to cook the rice. *Average cost*, 1s. 6d. *Sufficient* for 5 or 6 persons. *Seasonable* from August to March.

APPLES AND RICE (a pretty Dish of).

Ingredients.—6 oz. of rice, 1 quart of milk, the rind of ½ lemon, sugar to taste, ½ saltspoonful of salt, 8 apples, ¼ lb. of sugar, ¼ pint of water, ½ pint of boiled custard. *Mode.*—Flavour the milk with lemon-rind, by boiling them together for a few minutes; then take out the peel, and put in the rice, with sufficient sugar to sweeten it nicely, and boil gently until the rice is quite soft; then let it cool. In the meantime pare, quarter, and core the apples, and boil them until tender in a syrup made with sugar and water in the above proportion; and, when soft, lift them out on a sieve to drain. Now put a middling-sized gallipot in the centre of a dish; lay the rice all round till the top of the gallipot is reached; smooth the rice with the back of a spoon, and stick the apples into it in rows, one row sloping to the right, and the next to the left. Set it in the oven to colour the apples; then, when required for table, remove the gallipot, garnish the rice with preserved fruits, and pour in the middle sufficient custard, made by the recipe for boiled custard, to be level with the top of the rice, and serve hot. *Time.*—From 20 to 30 minutes to stew the apples; ¾ hour to simmer the rice; ¼ hour to bake. *Average cost*, 1s. 6d. *Sufficient* for 5 or 6 persons. *Seasonable* from August to March.

APPLES, Compôte of (Soyer's Recipe,—a Dessert Dish).

Ingredients.—6 ripe apples, 1 lemon, ½ lb. of lump sugar, ½ pint of water. *Mode.*—Select the apples of a moderate size, peel them, cut them in halves, remove the cores, and rub each piece over with a little lemon. Put the sugar and water together into a lined saucepan, and let them boil until forming a thickish syrup, when lay in the apples with the rind of the lemon cut thin, and the juice of the same. Let the apples simmer till tender; then take them out very carefully, drain them on a sieve, and reduce the syrup by boiling it quickly for a few minutes. When both are cold, arrange the apples neatly on a glass dish, pour over the syrup, and garnish with strips of green angelica or candied citron. Smaller apples may be dressed in the same manner: they should not be divided in half, but peeled, and the cores pushed out with a vegetable-cutter. *Time.*—10 minutes to boil the sugar and water together; from 20 to 30 minutes to simmer the apples. *Average cost, 6d. Sufficient* for 4 or 5 persons. *Seasonable* from August to March.

COMPÔTE OF APPLES.

APPLES, Flanc of; or Apples in a raised Crust. (Sweet Entremets.)

Ingredients.—¾ lb. of short crust, 9 moderate-sized apples, the rind and juice of ½ lemon, ½ lb. of white sugar, ¾ pint of water, a few strips of candied citron. *Mode.*—Make a plain stiff short crust, roll it out to the thickness of ½ inch, and butter an oval mould; line it with the crust, and press it carefully all round the sides, to obtain the form of the mould, but be particular not to break the paste. Pinch the part that just rises above the mould with the paste-pincers, and fill the case with flour; bake it for about ¾ hour; then take it out of the oven, remove the flour, put the case back in the oven for another ¼ hour, and do not allow it to get scorched. It is now ready for the apples, which should be prepared in the following manner: peel, and take out the cores with a small knife, or a scoop for the purpose, without dividing the apples; put them into a small lined saucepan, just capable of holding them, with sugar, water, lemon-juice and rind, in the above proportion. Simmer them very gently until tender; then take out the apples, let them cool, arrange them in the flanc or case, and boil down the syrup until reduced to a thick jelly; pour it over the apples, and garnish with a few slices of candied citron.

A more simple flanc may be made by rolling out the paste, cutting the bottom of a round or oval shape, and then a narrow strip for the sides: these should be stuck on with the white of an egg to the bottom piece, and the flanc then filled with raw fruit, with sufficient sugar to sweeten it nicely. It will not require so long baking as in a mould; but the crust must be made everywhere of an equal thickness, and so perfectly joined that the juice does not escape. This dish may also be served hot, and should be garnished in the same manner, or a little melted apricot jam may be poured over the apples, which very much improves their flavour. *Time.*—Altogether, 1 hour to bake the flanc; from 30 to 40 minutes to stew the apples very gently. *Average cost*, 1*s*. 6*d*. *Sufficient* for 1 entremets or side-dish. *Seasonable* from August to March.

APPLES, Ginger (a pretty Supper or Dessert Dish).

Ingredients.—1½ oz. of whole ginger, ¼ pint of whiskey, 3 lbs. of apples, 2 lbs. of white sugar, the juice of 2 lemons. *Mode.*—Bruise the ginger, put it into a small jar, pour over sufficient whiskey to cover it, and let it remain for 3 days; then cut the apples into thin slices, after paring and coring them; add the sugar and the lemon-juice, which should be strained; and simmer all together *very gently* until the apples are transparent, but not broken. Serve cold, and garnish the dish with slices of candied lemon-peel or preserved ginger. *Time.*—3 days to soak the ginger; about ¾ hour to simmer the apples very gently. *Average cost*, 2*s*. 6*d*. *Sufficient* for 3 dishes. *Seasonable* from August to March.

APPLES Iced, or Apple Hedgehog.

Ingredients.—About 3 dozen good boiling apples, 1 lb. of sugar, ½ pint of water, the rind of ½ lemon minced very fine, the whites of 2 eggs, 3 tablespoonfuls of pounded sugar, a few sweet almonds. *Mode.*—Peel and core a dozen of the apples without dividing them, and stew them very gently in a lined saucepan with ½ lb. of the sugar and ½ pint of water, and when tender lift them carefully on to a dish. Have ready the remainder of the apples, pared, cored, and cut into thin slices; put them into the same syrup with the other ½ lb. of sugar, the lemon-peel, and boil gently until they are reduced to a marmalade; keeping them stirred, to prevent them from burning. Cover the bottom of the dish with some of the marmalade, and over that a layer of the stewed apples, in the insides of which, and between each, place some of the marmalade; then place another layer of apples, and fill up the cavities with marmalade as before, forming the whole into a raised oval shape. Whip the whites of the eggs to a stiff froth, mix with them the pounded sugar, and cover the apples very smoothly all over with the icing; blanch and cut each almond into 4 or 5 strips; place these strips at equal distances over the icing, sticking up; strew over a little rough pounded sugar, and put the dish in a very slow oven, to colour the almonds, and so allow the apples to get warm through. This entremets may also be served cold, and makes a pretty supper-dish. *Time.*—From 20 to 30 minutes to stew the apples. *Averagecost*, 2*s.* to 2*s.* 6*d. Sufficient* for 5 or 6 persons. *Seasonable* from August to March.

APPLESinRedJelly(apr ettySupperDish).

Ingredients.—6 good-sized apples, 12 cloves, 6 oz. of pounded sugar, 1 lemon, 2 teacupfuls of water, 1 tablespoonful of gelatine, a few drops of prepared cochineal. *Mode.*—Choose rather large apples; peel them and take out the cores, either with a scoop or a small silver knife, and put into each apple 2 cloves and as much sifted sugar as they will hold. Place them, without touching each other, in a large pie-dish; add more white sugar, the juice of 1 lemon, and 2 teacupfuls of water. Bake in the oven, with a dish over them, until they are done. Look at them frequently, and, as each apple is cooked, place it in a glass dish. They must not be left in the oven after they are done, or they will break, and so would spoil the appearance of the dish. When the apples are neatly arranged in the dish without touching each other, strain the liquor in which they have been stewing into a lined saucepan; add to it the rind of the lemon, and a tablespoonful of gelatine which has been previously dissolved in cold water, and, if not sweet, a little more sugar, and 6 cloves. Boil till quite clear; colour with a few drops of prepared cochineal, and strain the jelly through a double muslin into a jug; let it cool a *little*; then pour it into the dish round the apples. When quite cold, garnish the tops of the apples with a bright-coloured marmalade, jelly, or the white of an egg beaten to a strong froth, with a little sifted sugar. *Time.*—From 30 to 50 minutes to bake the apples. *Average cost*, 1*s.*, with the garnishing. *Sufficient* for 4 or 5 persons. *Seasonable* from August to March.

APPLES,topr eserve,inQuarters(inimitationofGinger).

Ingredients.—To every lb. of apples allow ¾ lb. of sugar, 1½ oz. of the best white ginger; 1 oz. of ginger to every ½ pint of water. *Mode.*—Peel, core, and quarter the apples, and put the fruit, sugar, and ginger in layers into a wide-mouthed jar, and let them remain for 2 days; then infuse 1 oz. of ginger in ½ pint of boiling water, and cover it closely, and let it remain for 1 day: this quantity of ginger and water is for 3 lbs. of apples, with the other ingredients in proportion. Put the apples, &c., into a preserving-pan with the water strained from the ginger, and boil till the apples look clear and the syrup is rich, which will be in about an hour. The rind of a lemon may be added just before the apples have finished boiling; and great care must be taken not to break the pieces of apple in putting them into the jars. Serve on glass dishes for dessert. *Time.*—2 days for the apples to remain in the jar with sugar, &c.; 1 day to infuse the ginger; about 1 hour to boil the apples. *Average cost*, for 3 lbs. of apples, with the other ingredients in proportion, 2*s.* 3*d. Sufficient.*—3 lbs. should fill 3 moderate-sized jars. *Seasonable.*—This should be made in September, October, or November.

APPLES, Stewed, and Custard (a pretty Dish for a Juvenile Supper).

Ingredients.—7 good-sized apples, the rind of ½ lemon or 4 cloves, ½ lb. of sugar, ¾ pint of water, ½ pint of custard. *Mode.*—Pare and take out the cores of the apples, without dividing them, and, if possible, leave the stalks on; boil the sugar and water together for 10 minutes; then put in the apples with the lemon-rind or cloves, whichever flavour may be preferred, and simmer gently until they are tender, taking care not to let them break. Dish them neatly on a glass dish, reduce the syrup by boiling it quickly for a few minutes, let it cool a little; then pour it over the apples. Have ready quite ½ pint of custard made by the recipe for Boiled Custard; pour it round, but not over, the apples when they are quite cold, and the dish is ready for table. A few almonds blanched and cut into strips, and stuck in the apples, would improve their appearance. *Time.*—From 20 to 30 minutes to stew the apples. *Average cost*, 1*s. Sufficient* to fill a large glass dish. *Seasonable* from August to March.

APRICOT CREAM.

Ingredients.—12 to 16 ripe apricots, ½ lb. of sugar, 1½ pint of milk, the yolks of 8 eggs, 1 oz. of isinglass. *Mode.*—Divide the apricots, take out the stones, and boil them in a syrup made with ¼ lb. of sugar and ¼ pint of water, until they form a thin marmalade, which rub through a sieve. Boil the milk with the other ¼ lb. of sugar, let it cool a little, then mix with it the yolks of eggs which have been previously well beaten; put this mixture into a jug, place this jug in boiling water, and stir it one way over the fire until it thickens; but on no account let it boil. Strain through a sieve, add the isinglass, previously boiled with a small quantity of water, and keep stirring it till nearly cold; then mix the cream with the apricots; stir well, put it into an oiled mould, and, if convenient, set it on ice; at any rate, in a very cool place. It should turn out on the dish without any difficulty. In winter-time, when fresh apricots are not obtainable, a little jam may be substituted for them. *Time.*—From 20 to 30 minutes to boil the apricots. *Average cost*, 3*s.* 6*d.* *Sufficient* to fill a quart mould. *Seasonable* in August, September, and October.

APRICOT JAM, or Marmalade.

Ingredients.—To every lb. of ripe apricots, weighed after being skinned and stoned, allow 1 lb. of sugar. *Mode.*—Pare the apricots, which should be ripe, as thinly as possible, break them in half, and remove the stones. Weigh the fruit, and to every lb. allow the same proportion of loaf sugar. Pound the sugar very finely in a mortar, strew it over the apricots, which should be placed on dishes, and let them remain for 12 hours. Break the stones, blanch the kernels, and put them with the sugar and fruit into a preserving-pan. Let these simmer very gently until clear; take out the pieces of apricot singly as they become so, and, as fast as the scum rises, carefully remove it. Put the apricots into small jars, pour over them the syrup and kernels, cover the jam with pieces of paper dipped in the purest salad-oil, and stretch over the top of the jars tissue paper, cut about 2 inches larger and brushed over with the white of an egg: when dry, it will be perfectly hard and air-tight. *Time.*—12 hours, sprinkled with sugar; about ¾ hour to boil the jam. *Average cost.*—When cheap, apricots may be purchased for preserving at about 1*s.* 6*d.* per gallon. *Sufficient.*—10 lbs. of fruit for 12 pots of jam. *Seasonable.*—Make this in August or September.

APRICOT PUDDING, Baked.

Ingredients.—12 large apricots, ¾ pint of bread-crumbs, 1 pint of milk, 3 oz. of pounded sugar, the yolks of 4 eggs, 1 glass of sherry. *Mode.*—Make the milk boiling hot, and pour it on to the bread-crumbs; when half cold, add the sugar, the well-whisked yolks of the eggs, and the sherry. Divide the apricots in half, scald them until they are soft, and break them up with a spoon, adding a few of the kernels, which should be well pounded in a mortar; then mix the fruit and other ingredients together, put a border of paste round the dish, fill with the mixture, and bake the pudding from ½ to ¾ hour. *Time.*—½ to ¾ hour. *Average cost*, in full season, 1*s*. 6*d*. *Sufficient* for 4 or 5 persons. *Seasonable* in August, September, and October.

APRICOT TART.

Ingredients.—12 or 14 apricots, sugar to taste, puff-paste or short crust. *Mode.*—Break the apricots in half, take out the stones, and put them into a pie-dish, in the centre of which place a very small cup or jar, bottom uppermost; sweeten with good moist sugar, but add no water. Line the edge of the dish with paste, put on the cover, and ornament the pie in any of the usual modes. Bake from ½ to ¾ hour, according to size; and if puff-paste is used, glaze it about 10 minutes before the pie is done, and put it into the oven again to set the glaze. Short crust merely requires a little sifted sugar sprinkled over it before being sent to table. Green apricots make very good tarts, but they should be boiled with a little sugar and water before they are covered with the crust. *Time.*—½ to ¾ hour. *Average cost*, in full season, 1*s*. *Sufficient* for 4 or 5 persons. *Seasonable* in August, September, and October; green ones rather earlier.

APRICOTS, Compôte of (an elegant Dish).

Ingredients.—½ pint of syrup (*see* Syrup), 12 green apricots. *Mode.*—Make the syrup by the given recipe, and, when it is ready, put in the apricots whilst the syrup is boiling. Simmer them very gently until tender, taking care not to let them break; take them out carefully, arrange them on a glass dish, let the syrup cool a little, pour it over the apricots, and, when cold, serve. *Time.*—From 15 to 20 minutes to simmer the apricots. *Average cost*, 9*d*. *Sufficient* for 4 or 5 persons. *Seasonable* in June and July, with green apricots.

APRICOTS, Flanc of, or Compôte of Apricots in a Raised Crust (Sweet Entremets).

Ingredients.—¾ lb. of short crust (*see* Crust), from 9 to 12 good-sized apricots, ¾ pint of water, ½ lb. of sugar. *Mode.*—Make a short crust by the given recipe, and line a mould with it. Boil the sugar and water together for 10 minutes; halve the apricots, take out the stones, and simmer them in the syrup until tender; watch them carefully, and take them up, for fear they should break. Arrange them neatly in the flanc or case; boil the syrup until reduced to a jelly; pour it over the fruit, and serve either hot or cold. Greengages, plums of all kinds, peaches, &c., may be done in the same manner, as also currants, raspberries, gooseberries, strawberries, &c.; but with the last-named fruits, a little currant-juice added to them will be found an improvement. *Time.*—Altogether, 1 hour to bake the flanc, from 15 to 20 minutes to simmer the apricots. *Average cost*, 1*s*. 6*d*. *Sufficient* for 1 entremets or side-dish. *Seasonable* in July, August, and September.

The pretty appearance of this dish depends on the fruit being whole; as each apricot is done, it should be taken out of the syrup immediately.

APRIL—BILLS OF FARE.

Dinner for 18 persons.

First Course.

Fillets of Mackerel.	Spring Soup, removed by Salmon and Lobster Sauce. Vase of Flowers Soles à la Crême.	Fried Smelts.

Second Course.

Stewed Beef à la Jardinière.	Roast Ribs of Lamb. Larded Capon. Vase of Flowers. Spring Chickens. Braised Turkey.	Boiled Ham.

Entrées.

Curried Lobster.	Lamb Cutlets, Asparagus and Peas. Vase of Flowers. Grenadines de Veau.	Oyster Patties.

Third Course.

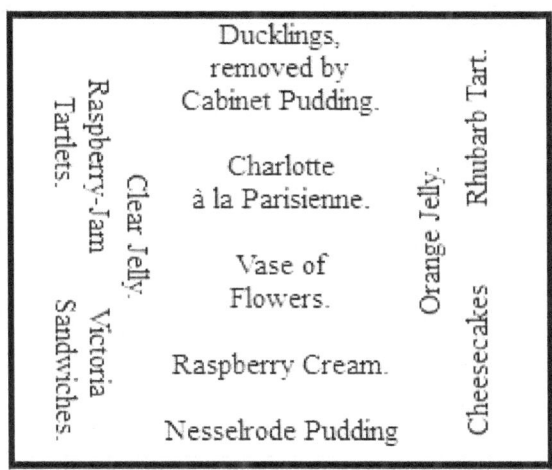

Dessert and Ices.

Dinner for 12 persons.

First Course.—Soup à la reine; julienne soup; turbot and lobster sauce; slices of salmon à la genévése. *Entrées.*—Croquettes of leveret; fricandeau de veau; vol-au-vent; stewed mushrooms. *Second Course.*—Fore-quarter of lamb; saddle of mutton; boiled chickens, asparagus and peas; boiled tongue garnished with tufts of broccoli; vegetables. *Third Course.*—Ducklings; larded guinea-fowls; charlotte à la parisienne; orange jelly; meringues; ratafia ice pudding; lobster salad; sea-kale; dessert and ices.

Dinner for 10 persons.

First Course.—Gravy soup; salmon and dressed cucumber; shrimp sauce; fillets of whitings. *Entrées.*—Lobster cutlets; chicken patties. *Second Course.*—Roast fillet of veal; boiled leg of lamb; ham, garnished with broccoli; vegetables. *Third Course.*—Ducklings; compôte of rhubarb; custards; vanilla cream; orange jelly; cabinet pudding; ice pudding; dessert.

Dinner for 8 persons.

First Course.—Spring soup; slices of salmon and caper sauce; fried filleted soles. *Entrées.*—Chicken vol-au-vent; mutton cutlets and tomato sauce. *Second Course.*—Roast loin of veal; boiled fowls à la béchamel; tongue; vegetables. *Third Course.*—Guinea-fowls; sea-kale; artichoke bottoms; cabinet pudding; blancmange; apricot tartlets; rice fritters; macaroni and Parmesan cheese; dessert.

Dinners for 6 persons.

First Course.—Tapioca soup; boiled salmon and lobster sauce. *Entrées.*—Sweetbreads; oyster patties. *Second Course.*—Haunch of mutton; boiled capon and white sauce; tongue; vegetables. *Third Course.*—Soufflé of rice; lemon cream; charlotte à la parisienne; rhubarb tart; dessert.

First Course.—Julienne soup; fried whitings; red mullet. *Entrées.*—Lamb cutlets and cucumbers; rissoles. *Second Course.*—Roast ribs of beef; neck of veal à la béchamel; vegetables. *Third Course.*—Ducklings; lemon pudding; rhubarb tart; custards; cheesecakes; dessert.

First Course.—Vermicelli soup; brill and shrimp sauce. *Entrées.*—Fricandeau of veal; lobster cutlets. *Second Course.*—Roast fore-quarter of lamb; boiled chickens; tongue; vegetables. *Third Course.*—Goslings; sea-kale; plum pudding; whipped cream; compôte of rhubarb; cheesecakes; dessert.

First Course.—Ox-tail soup; crimped salmon. *Entrées.*—Croquettes of chicken; mutton cutlets and soubise sauce. *Second Course.*—Roast fillet of veal; boiled bacon-cheek, garnished with sprouts; boiled capon; vegetables. *Third Course.*—Sea-kale; lobster salad; cabinet pudding; ginger cream; raspberry-jam tartlets; rhubarb tart; macaroni; dessert.

APRIL, Plain Family Dinners for.

Sunday.—1. Clear gravy soup. 2. Roast haunch of mutton, sea-kale, potatoes. 3. Rhubarb tart, custards in glasses.

Monday.—1. Crimped skate and caper sauce. 2. Boiled knuckle of veal and rice, cold mutton, mashed potatoes. 3. Baked plum-pudding.

Tuesday.—1. Vegetable soup. 2. Toad-in-the-hole, made from remains of cold mutton. 3. Stewed rhubarb and baked custard puddings.

Wednesday.—1. Fried soles, anchovy sauce. 2. Boiled beef and carrots, suet dumplings. 3. Lemon pudding.

Thursday.—1. Pea-soup, made with liquor that beef was boiled in. 2. Cold beef, mashed potatoes, mutton cutlets and tomato sauce. 3. Macaroni.

Friday.—1. Bubble-and-squeak made with remains of cold beef, roast shoulder of veal stuffed, spinach and potatoes. 2. Boiled batter pudding and sweet sauce.

Saturday.—1. Stewed veal with vegetables, made of remains of cold shoulder, broiled rump-steak and oyster sauce. 2. Yeast dumplings.

Sunday.—Boiled salmon and dressed cucumber, anchovy sauce. 2. Roast fore-quarter of lamb, spinach, potatoes, and mint sauce. 3. Rhubarb tart and cheesecakes.

Monday.—Curried salmon, made with remains of salmon, dish of boiled rice. 2. Cold lamb, rump-steak and kidney pudding, potatoes. 3. Spinach and poached eggs.

Tuesday.—1. Scotch mutton broth with pearl barley. 2. Boiled neck of mutton, caper sauce, suet dumplings, carrots. 3. Baked rice puddings.

Wednesday.—1. Boiled mackerel and melted butter and fennel sauce, potatoes. 2. Roast fillet of veal, bacon and greens. 3. Fig pudding.

Thursday.—1. Flemish soup. 2. Roast loin of mutton, broccoli, potatoes, veal rolls made from remains of cold veal. 3. Boiled rhubarb pudding.

Friday.—1. Irish stew or haricot for cold mutton, minced veal. 2. Half-pay pudding.

Saturday.—1. Rump-steak pie, broiled mutton chops. 2. Baked arrowroot pudding.

APRIL, Things in Season.

Fish.—Brill, carp, cockles, crabs, dory, flounders, ling, lobsters, red and grey mullet, mussels, oysters, perch, prawns, salmon (but rather scarce and expensive), shad, shrimps, skate, smelts, soles, tench, turbot, whitings.

Meat.—Beef, lamb, mutton, veal.

Poultry.—Chickens, ducklings, fowls, pigeons, pullets, rabbits.

Game.—Leverets.

Vegetables.—Broccoli, celery, lettuces, young onions, parsnips, radishes, small salad, sea-kale, spinach, sprouts, various herbs.

Fruit.—Apples, nuts, pears, forced cherries, &c. for tarts, rhubarb, dried fruits, crystallized preserves.

ARROWROOT BISCUITS, or Drops.

Ingredients.—½ lb. of butter, 6 eggs, ½ lb. of flour, 6 oz. of arrowroot, ½ lb. of pounded loaf sugar. *Mode.*—Beat the butter to a cream; whisk the eggs to a strong froth, add them to the butter, stir in the flour a little at a time, and beat the mixture well. Break down all the lumps from the arrowroot, and add that with the sugar to the other ingredients. Mix all well together, drop the dough on a buttered tin, in pieces the size of a shilling, and bake the biscuits about ¼ hour in a slow oven. If the whites of the eggs are separated from the yolks, and both are beaten separately before being added to the other ingredients, the biscuits will be much lighter. *Time.*—¼ hour. *Average cost*, 2s. 6d. *Sufficient* to make from 3 to 4 dozen biscuits. *Seasonable* at any time.

ARROWROOT BLANCMANGE (an inexpensive Supper Dish).

Ingredients.—4 heaped tablespoonfuls of arrowroot, 1½ pint of milk, 3 laurel-leaves or the rind of ½ lemon, sugar to taste. *Mode.*—Mix to a smooth batter the arrowroot with ½ pint of the milk; put the other pint on the fire, with laurel-leaves or lemon-peel, whichever may be preferred, and let the milk steep until it is well flavoured; then strain the milk, and add it, boiling, to the mixed arrowroot; sweeten it with sifted sugar, and let it boil, stirring it all the time, till it thickens sufficiently to come from the saucepan. Grease a mould with pure salad-oil, pour in the blancmange, and, when quite set, turn it out on a dish, and pour round it a compôte of any kind of fruit, or garnish it with jam. A tablespoonful of brandy, stirred in just before the blancmange is moulded, very much improves the flavour of this sweet dish. *Time.*—Altogether, ½ hour. *Average cost*, 6d. without the garnishing. *Sufficient* for 4 or 5 persons. *Seasonable* at any time.

ARROWROOT PUDDING, Baked or Boiled.

Ingredients.—2 tablespoonfuls of arrowroot, 1½ pint of milk, 1 oz. of butter, the rind of ½ lemon, 2 heaped tablespoonfuls of moist sugar, a little grated nutmeg. *Mode.*—Mix the arrowroot with as much cold milk as will make it into a smooth batter, moderately thick; put the remainder of the milk into a stewpan with the lemon-peel, and let it infuse for about ½ hour; when it boils, strain it gently to the batter, stirring it all the time to keep it smooth; then add the butter; beat this well in until thoroughly mixed, and sweeten with moist sugar. Put the mixture into a pie-dish, round which has been placed a border of paste; grate a little nutmeg over the top, and bake the pudding from 1 to 1¼ hour, in a moderate oven, or boil it the same length of time in a well-buttered basin. To enrich this pudding, stir to the other ingredients, just before it is put in the oven, 3 well-whisked eggs, and add a tablespoonful of brandy. For a nursery pudding, the addition of the latter ingredients will be found quite superfluous, as also the paste round the edge of the dish. *Time.*—1 to 1¼ hour, baked or boiled. *Average cost*, 7d. *Sufficient* for 5 or 6 persons. *Seasonable* at any time.

ARROWROOT SAUCE, for Puddings.

Ingredients.—2 small teaspoonfuls of arrowroot, 4 dessertspoonfuls of pounded sugar, the juice of 1 lemon, ¼ teaspoonful of grated nutmeg, ½ pint of water. *Mode.*—Mix the arrowroot smoothly with the water; put this into a stewpan; add the sugar, strained lemon-juice, and grated nutmeg. Stir these ingredients over the fire until they boil, when the sauce is ready for use. A small quantity of wine, or any liqueur, would very much improve the flavour of this sauce: it is usually served with bread, rice, custard, or any dry pudding that is not very rich. *Time.*—Altogether, 15 minutes. *Average cost*, 4d. *Sufficient* for 6 or 7 persons.

ARROWROOT, to make.

Ingredients.—Two teaspoonfuls of arrowroot, 3 tablespoonfuls of cold water, ½ pint of boiling water. *Mode.*—Mix the arrowroot smoothly in a basin with the cold water, then pour on it the *boiling* water, *stirring* all the time. The water must be *boiling* at the time it is poured on the mixture, or it will not thicken; if mixed with hot water only, it must be put into a clean saucepan, and boiled until it thickens; but this occasions more trouble, and is quite unnecessary, if the water is boiling at first. Put the arrowroot into a tumbler, sweeten it with lump sugar, and flavour it with grated nutmeg or cinnamon, or a piece of lemon-peel, or, when allowed, 3 tablespoonfuls of port or sherry. As arrowroot is in itself flavourless and insipid, it is almost necessary to add the wine to make it palatable. Arrowroot made with milk instead of water is far nicer, but is not so easily digested. It should be mixed in the same manner, with 3 tablespoonfuls of cold water, the boiling milk then poured on it, and well stirred. When made in this manner, no wine should be added, but merely sugar, and a little grated nutmeg or lemon-peel. *Time.*—If obliged to be boiled, 2 minutes. *Average cost*, 2d. per pint. *Sufficient* to make ½ pint of arrowroot.

ARTICHOKES, Boiled.

Ingredients.—To each ½ gallon of water, allow 1 heaped tablespoonful of salt, a piece of soda the size of a shilling; artichokes. *Mode.*—Wash the artichokes well in several waters; see that no insects remain about them, and trim away the leaves at the bottom. Cut off the stems and put them into *boiling* water, to which has been added salt and soda in the above proportion. Keep the saucepan uncovered, and let them boil quickly until tender; ascertain when they are done by thrusting a fork in them, or by trying if the leaves can be easily removed. Take them out, let them drain for a minute or two, and serve in a napkin, or with a little white sauce poured over. A tureen of melted butter should accompany them. This vegetable, unlike any other, is considered better for being gathered two or three days;

but they must be well soaked and washed previous to dressing. *Time.*—20 to 25 minutes, after the water boils. *Sufficient,*—a dish of 5 or 6 for 4 persons. *Seasonable* from July to the beginning of September.

ARTICHOKES.

ARTICHOKES, a French Mode of Cooking.

Ingredients.—5 or 6 artichokes; to each ½ gallon of water allow 1 heaped tablespoonful of salt, ½ teaspoonful of pepper, 1 bunch of savoury herbs, 2 oz. of butter. *Mode.*—Cut the ends of the leaves, as also the stems; put the artichokes into boiling water, with the above proportion of salt, pepper, herbs, and butter; let them boil quickly until tender, keeping the lid of the saucepan off, and when the leaves come out easily, they are cooked enough. To keep them a beautiful green, put a large piece of cinder into a muslin bag, and let it boil with them. Serve with plain melted butter. *Time.*—20 to 25 minutes. *Sufficient,*—5 or 6 sufficient for 4 or 5 persons. *Seasonable* from July to the beginning of September.

JERUSALEM ARTICHOKES.

ARTICHOKES. Fried (Entremets, or small dish to be served with the Second Course).

Ingredients.—5 or 6 artichokes, salt and water: for the batter,—¼ lb. of flour, a little salt, the yolk of 1 egg, milk. *Mode.*—Trim and boil the artichokes, and rub them over with lemon-juice, to keep them white. When they are quite tender, take them up, remove the chokes, and divide the bottoms; dip each piece into batter, fry them into hot lard or dripping, and garnish the dish with crisped parsley. Serve with plain melted butter. *Time.*—20 minutes to boil the artichokes, 5 to 7 minutes to fry them. *Sufficient,*—

5 or 6 for 4 or 5 persons. *Seasonable* from July to the beginning of September.

ARTICHOKES à l'Italienne.

Ingredients.—4 or 5 artichokes, salt and butter, about ½ pint of good gravy. *Mode.*—Trim and cut the artichokes into quarters, and boil them until tender in water mixed with a little salt and butter. When done, drain them well, and lay them all round the dish, with the leaves outside. Have ready some good gravy, highly flavoured with mushrooms; reduce it until quite thick, and pour it round the artichokes, and serve. *Time.*—20 to 25 minutes to boil the artichokes. *Sufficient* for one side-dish. *Seasonable* from July to the beginning of September.

ARTICHOKES, Boiled Jerusalem.

Ingredients.—To each ½ gallon of water allow 1 heaped tablespoonful of salt; artichokes. *Mode.*—Wash, peel, and shape the artichokes in a round or oval form, and put them into a saucepan with sufficient *cold* water to cover them salted in the above proportion. Let them boil gently until tender; take them up, drain them, and serve them in a napkin, or plain, whichever mode is preferred; send to table with them a tureen of melted butter or cream sauce, a little of which may be poured over the artichokes when they are *not* served in a napkin. *Time.*—About twenty minutes after the water boils. *Average cost*, 2*d.* per lb. *Sufficient,*—10 for a dish for 6 persons. *Seasonable.*—from September to June.

ARTICHOKES, Mashed Jerusalem.

Ingredients.—To each ½ gallon of water allow 1 oz. of salt, 15 or 16 artichokes, 1 oz. butter, pepper and salt to taste. *Mode.*—Boil the artichokes as in the preceding recipe until tender; drain and press the water from them, and beat them up with a fork. When thoroughly mashed and free from lumps, put them into a saucepan with the butter and a seasoning of *white* pepper and salt; keep stirring over the fire until the artichokes are quite hot, and serve. A pretty way of serving Jerusalem artichokes as an entremets, or second course dish, is to shape the artichokes in the form of a pear, and to serve them covered with white sauce, garnished with Brussels sprouts.

Time.—About 20 minutes. *Average cost,* 2*d.* per lb. *Sufficient* for 6 or 7 persons. *Seasonable* from September to June.

ARTICHOKE (Jerusalem) SOUP, sometimes called Palestine Soup (a White Soup).

Ingredients.—3 slices of lean bacon or ham, ½ a head of celery, 1 turnip, 1 onion, 3 oz. of butter, 4 lbs. of artichokes, 1 pint of boiling milk, or 1 pint of boiling cream, salt and cayenne to taste, 2 lumps of sugar, 2½ quarts of white stock. *Mode.*—Put the bacon and vegetables, which should be cut into thin slices, into the stewpan with the butter. Braise these for ¼ of an hour, keeping them well stirred. Wash and pare the artichokes, and after cutting them into thin slices, add them, with a pint of stock, to the other ingredients. When these have gently stewed down to a smooth pulp, put in the remainder of the stock. Stir it well, adding the seasoning, and when it has simmered for five minutes, pass it through a strainer. Now pour it back into the stewpan, let it again simmer five minutes, taking care to skim it well, and stir it to the boiling milk or cream. Serve with small sippets of bread fried in butter. *Time.*—1 hour. *Average cost* per quart, 1*s.* 2*d.* *Seasonable* from June to October. *Sufficient* for 8 persons.

BOILED ASPARAGUS.

ASPARAGUS, Boiled.

Ingredients.—To each ½ gallon of water allow 1 heaped tablespoonful of salt; asparagus. *Mode.*—Asparagus should be dressed as soon as possible after it is cut, although it may be kept for a day or two by putting the stalks into cold water; yet to be good, like every other vegetable, it cannot be cooked too fresh. Scrape the white part of the stems, *beginning* from the *head,* and throw them into cold water; then tie them into bundles of about 20 each, keeping the heads all one way, and cut the stalks evenly, that they may all be the same length; put them into *boiling* water, with salt in the above proportion; keep them boiling quickly until tender, with the saucepan uncovered. When the asparagus is done, dish it upon toast, which should be dipped in the water it was cooked in, and leave the white ends outward each way, with the points meeting in the middle. Serve with a tureen of melted butter. *Time.*—15 to 18 minutes after the water boils. *Average cost,* in full season, 2*s.* 6*d.* the 100 heads. *Sufficient.*—Allow about 50 heads for 4 or 5 persons. *Seasonable.*—May be had forced from January, but cheapest in May, June and July.

ASPARAGUS TONGS.

ASPARAGUS-PEAS (Entremets, or to be served as a Side Dish, with the Second Course).

Ingredients.—100 heads of asparagus, 2 oz. of butter, a small bunch of parsley, 2 or 3 green onions, flour, 1 lump of sugar, the yolks of 2 eggs, 4 tablespoonfuls of cream, salt. *Mode.*—Carefully scrape the asparagus, cut it into pieces of an equal size, avoiding that which is in the least hard or tough, and throw them into cold water. Then boil the asparagus in salt and water until three-parts done; take it out, drain, and place it on a cloth to dry the moisture away from it. Put it into a stewpan with the butter, parsley, and onions, and shake over a brisk fire for 10 minutes. Dredge in a little flour, add the sugar, and moisten with boiling water. When boiled a short time and reduced, take out the parsley and onions, thicken with the yolks of 2 eggs beaten with the cream; add a seasoning of salt, and when the whole is on the point of simmering, serve. Make the sauce sufficiently thick to adhere to the vegetable. *Time.*—Altogether, ½ hour. *Average cost*, 1*s.* 6*d.* a pint. *Seasonable* in May, June, and July.

ASPARAGUS PUDDING (a delicious Dish, to be served with the Second Course).

Ingredients.—½ pint of asparagus peas, 4 eggs, 2 tablespoonfuls of flour, 1 tablespoonful of *very finely* minced ham, 1 oz. of butter, pepper and salt to taste, milk. *Mode.*—Cut up the nice green tender parts of asparagus, about the size of peas; put them into a basin with the eggs, which should be well beaten, and the flour, ham, butter, pepper, and salt. Mix all these ingredients well together, and moisten with sufficient milk to make the pudding of the consistency of thick batter; put it into a pint buttered mould, tie it down tightly with a floured cloth, place it in *boiling water*, and let it boil for 2 hours; turn it out of the mould on to a hot dish, and pour plain melted butter *round*, but not over, the pudding. Green peas pudding may be made in exactly the same manner, substituting peas for the asparagus. *Time.*—2 hours. *Average cost*, 1*s*. 6*d*. per pint. *Seasonable* in May, June, and July.

ASPARAGUS SOUP.

Ingredients.—100 heads of asparagus, 2 quarts of medium stock (see STOCK), 1 pint of water, salt. *Mode.*—Scrape the asparagus, but do not cut off any of the stems, and boil it in a pint of water salted, *until the heads are nearly done*. Then drain the asparagus, cut off the green heads very neatly, and put them on one side until the soup is ready. If the stock is not made, add the stems of asparagus to the rest of the vegetables; if, however, the stock is ready, boil the stems a little longer in the same water that they were first cooked in. Then strain them off, add the asparagus water to the stock, and when all is boiling drop in the green heads (or peas as they are called), and simmer for 2 or 3 minutes. If the soup boils long after the asparagus is put in, the appearance of the vegetable would be quite spoiled. A small quantity of sherry, added after the soup is put into the tureen, would improve this soup very much. Sometimes a French roll is cut up and served in it. *Time.*—*To nearly cook* the asparagus, 12 minutes. *Average cost*, 1*s*. 9*d*. per quart. *Sufficient* for 6 or 8 persons. *Seasonable* from May to August.

ASPIC, or Ornamental Savoury Jelly.

Ingredients.—4 lbs. of knuckle of veal, 1 cow-heel, 3 or 4 slices of ham, any poultry trimmings, 2 carrots, 1 onion, 1 faggot of savoury herbs, 1 glass of sherry, 3 quarts of water; seasoning to taste of salt and whole white pepper; 3 eggs. *Mode.*—Lay the ham on the bottom of a stewpan, cut up the veal and cow-heel into small pieces, and lay them on the ham; add the poultry trimmings, vegetables, herbs, sherry, and water, and let the whole simmer very gently for 4 hours, carefully taking away all scum that may rise to the surface; strain through a fine sieve, and pour into an earthen pan to get cold. Have ready a clean stewpan, put in the jelly, and be particular to leave the sediment behind, or it will not be clear. Add the whites of 3 eggs, with salt and pepper, to clarify; keep stirring over the fire till the whole becomes very white; then draw it to the side, and let it stand till clear. When this is the case, strain it through a cloth or jelly-bag, and use it for moulding poultry, &c. Tarragon vinegar may be added to give an additional flavour. *Time.*—Altogether 4½ hours. *Average cost* for this quantity, 4s.

AUGUST—BILLS OF FARE.

Dinner for 18 persons.

First Course.

Red Mullet.	Mock-Turtle Soup, removed by Broiled Salmon and Caper Sauce. Vase of Flowers. Soup à la Julienne, removed by Brill and Shrimp Sauce.	Perch.

Second Course.

Capons à la Financière.	Haunch of Venison. Ham, garnished. Vase of Flowers. Leveret Pie. Saddle of Mutton.	Roast Fowls.

Entrées.

```
┌─────────────────────────────────────┐
│                  Fricandeau de Veau │
│                    à la Jardinière. │
│  C                                  L
│  u                                  a
│  r                                  m
│  r                Vase of           b
│  i                Flowers.          C
│  e                                  u
│  d                                  t
│                                     l
│  L                                  e
│  o                Fillets of Ducks  t
│  b                and Peas.         s
│  s                                  …
│  t                                  
│  e                                  
│  r                                  
└─────────────────────────────────────┘
```

Third Course.

```
┌─────────────────────────────────────┐
│                  Grouse             │
│                  removed by         │
│                  Cabinet Pudding.   │
│  L                                  C
│  o                                  h
│  b    C           Fruit Jelly.      e
│  s    h                             e
│  t    a                          C  s
│  e    r                          u  e
│  r    l           Vase of        s  c
│       o           Flowers.       t  a
│  S    t                          a  k
│  a    t                          r  e
│  l    e           Vol-au-Vent of d  s
│  a    …           Pears.         s  …
│  d    …                          …  
│       R                             
│       a                             P
│       s           Larded Peahen,    r
│       p           removed by        a
│       b           Iced Pudding.     w
│       …                             n
│                                     s
└─────────────────────────────────────┘
```

Dessert and Ices.

Dinner for 12 persons.

First Course.—Vermicelli soup; soup à la reine; boiled salmon; fried flounders; trout en matelot. *Entrées.*—Stewed pigeons; sweetbreads; ragoût of ducks; fillets of chickens and mushrooms. *Second Course.*—Quarter of lamb; cotellette de bœuf à la jardinière; roast fowls and boiled tongue; bacon and beans. *Third Course.*—Grouse; wheatears; greengage tart; whipped cream; vol-au-vent of plums; fruit jelly; iced pudding; cabinet pudding; dessert and ices.

Dinner for 8 persons.

First Course.—Julienne soup; fillets of turbot and Dutch sauce; red mullet. *Entrées.*—Riz de veau aux tomates; fillets of ducks and peas. *Second Course.*—Haunch of venison; boiled capon and oysters; ham, garnished; vegetables. *Third Course.*—Leveret; fruit jelly; compôte of greengages; plum tart; custards, in glasses; omelette soufflé; dessert and ices.

Dinner for 6 persons.

First Course.—Macaroni soup; crimped salmon and sauce Hollandaise; fried fillets of trout. *Entrées.*—Tendrons do veau and stewed peas; salmi of grouse. *Second Course.*—Roast loin of veal; boiled bacon, garnished with French beans; stewed beef à la jardinière; vegetables. *Third Course.*—Turkey poult; plum tart; custard pudding; vol-au-vent of pears; strawberry cream; ratafia soufflé; dessert.

First Course.—Vegetable-marrow soup; stewed mullet; fillets of salmon and ravigotte sauce. *Entrées.*—Curried lobster; fricandeau de veau à la jardinière. *Second Course.*—Roast saddle of mutton; stewed shoulder of veal, garnished with forcemeat balls; vegetables. *Third Course.*—Roast grouse and bread sauce; vol-au-vent of greengages; fruit jelly; raspberry cream; custards; fig pudding; dessert.

AUGUST, Plain Family Dinners for.

Sunday.—1. Vegetable-marrow soup. 2. Roast quarter of lamb, mint sauce; French beans and potatoes. 3. Raspberry-and-currant tart, custard pudding.

Monday.—1. Cold lamb and salad, small meat-pie, vegetable marrow, and white sauce. 2. Lemon dumplings.

Tuesday.—1. Boiled mackerel. 2. Stewed loin of veal, French beans and potatoes, 3. Baked raspberry pudding.

Wednesday.—1. Vegetable soup. 2. Lamb cutlets and French beans; the remains of stewed shoulder of veal, mashed vegetable marrow. 3. Black-currant pudding.

Thursday.—1. Roast ribs of beef, Yorkshire pudding, French beans and potatoes. 2. Bread-and-butter pudding.

Friday.—1. Fried soles and melted butter. 2. Cold beef and salad, lamb cutlets and mashed potatoes. 3. Cauliflowers and white sauce instead of pudding.

Saturday.—1. Stewed beef and vegetables, with remains of cold beef; mutton pudding. 2. Macaroni and cheese.

Sunday.—1. Salmon pudding. 2. Roast fillet of veal, boiled bacon-cheek garnished with tufts of cauliflowers, French beans and potatoes. 3. Plum tart, boiled custard pudding.

Monday.—1. Baked soles. 2. Cold veal and bacon, salad, mutton cutlets and tomato sauce. 3. Boiled currant pudding.

Tuesday.—1. Rice soup. 2. Roast fowls and water-cresses, boiled knuckle of ham, minced veal garnished with croûtons; vegetables. 3. College pudding.

Wednesday.—1. Curried fowl with remains of cold fowl; dish of rice, stewed rump-steak and vegetables. 2. Plum tart.

Thursday.—1. Boiled brisket of beef, carrots, turnips, suet dumplings, and potatoes. 2. Baked bread pudding.

Friday.—1. Vegetable soup, made from liquor that beef was boiled in. 2. Cold beef and dressed cucumber, veal cutlets and tomato sauce. 3. Fondue.

Saturday.—1. Bubble-and-squeak, made from remains of cold beef; cold veal-and-ham pie, salad. 2. Baked raspberry pudding.

AUGUST, Things in Season.

Fish.—Brill, carp, chub, crayfish, crabs, dory, eels, flounders, grigs, herrings, lobsters, mullet, pike, prawns, salmon, shrimps, skate, soles, sturgeon, thornback, trout, turbot.

Meat.—Beef, lamb, mutton, veal, buck venison.

Poultry.—Chickens, ducklings, fowls, green geese, pigeons, plovers, pullets, rabbits, turkey poults, wheatears, wild ducks.

Game.—Leverets, grouse, black-cock.

Vegetables.—Artichokes, asparagus, beans, carrots, cabbages, cauliflowers, celery, cresses, endive, lettuces, mushrooms, onions, peas, potatoes, radishes, sea-kale, small salading, sprouts, turnips, various kitchen herbs, vegetable marrows.

Fruit.—Currants, figs, filberts, gooseberries, grapes, melons, mulberries, nectarines, peaches, pears, pineapples, plums, raspberries, walnuts.

BACON, Boiled.

Ingredients.—Bacon; water. *Mode.*—As bacon is frequently excessively salt, let it be soaked in warm water for an hour or two previous to dressing it; then pare off the rusty parts, and scrape the under-side and rind as clean as possible. Put it into a saucepan of cold water; let it come gradually to a boil, and as fast as the scum rises to the surface of the water, remove it. Let it simmer very gently until it is *thoroughly* done; then take it up, strip off the skin, and sprinkle over the bacon a few bread raspings, and garnish with tufts of cauliflower or Brussels sprouts. When served alone, young and tender broad beans or green peas are the usual accompaniments. *Time.*—1 lb. of bacon, ¾ hour; 2 lbs., 1½ hour. *Average cost,* 10*d.* to 1*s.* per lb. for the primest parts. *Sufficient.*—2 lbs., when served with poultry or veal, sufficient for 10 persons. *Seasonable* at any time.

BOILED BACON.

BACON, Broiled Rashers of.

Before purchasing bacon, ascertain that it is perfectly free from rust, which may easily be detected by its yellow colour; and for broiling, the streaked part of the thick flank is generally the most esteemed. Cut it into *thin* slices, take off the rind, and broil over a nice clear fire; turn it two or three times, and serve very hot. Should there be any cold bacon left from the previous day, it answers very well for breakfast, cut into slices, and broiled or fried. *Time.*—3 or 4 minutes. *Average cost,* 10*d.* to 1*s.* per lb. for the primest parts. *Seasonable* at any time.

Note.—When the bacon is cut very thin, the slices may be curled round and fastened by means of small skewers, and fried or toasted before the fire.

BACON and HAMS, Curing of.

The carcass of the hog, after hanging over-night to cool, is laid on a strong bench or stool, and the head is separated from the body at the neck close behind the ears; the feet and also the internal fat are removed. The carcass is next divided into two sides in the following manner:—The ribs are divided about an inch from the spine on each side, and the spine, with the ends of the ribs attached, together with the internal flesh between it and the kidneys, and also the flesh above it, throughout the whole length of the sides, are removed. The portion of the carcass thus cut out is in the form of a wedge—the breadth of the interior consisting of the breadth of the spine, and about an inch of the ribs on each side, being diminished to about half an inch at the exterior or skin along the back. The breastbone, and also the first anterior rib, are also dissected from the side. Sometimes the whole of the ribs are removed; but this, for reasons afterwards to be noticed, is a very bad practice. When the hams are cured separately from the sides, which is generally the case, they are cut out so as to include the hock-bone, in a similar manner to the London mode of cutting a haunch of mutton. The carcass of the hog thus cut up is ready for being salted, which process, in large curing establishments, is generally as follows:—The skin side of the pork is rubbed over with a mixture of fifty parts by weight of salt, and one part of saltpetre in powder, and the incised parts of the ham or flitch, and the inside of the flitch, covered with the same. The salted bacon, in pairs of flitches with the insides to each other, is piled one pair of flitches above another on benches slightly inclined, and furnished with spouts or troughs to convey the brine to receivers in the floor of the salting-house, to be afterwards used for pickling pork for navy purposes. In this state the bacon remains a fortnight, which is sufficient for flitches cut from hogs of a carcass weight less than 15 stone (14 lbs. to the stone). Flitches of a larger size, at the expiration of that time, are wiped dry and reversed in their place in the pile, having, at the same time, about half the first quantity of fresh, dry, common salt sprinkled over the inside and incised parts; after which they remain on the benches for another week. Hams being thicker than flitches, will require, when less than 20 lbs. weight, 3 weeks; and when above that weight, 4 weeks to remain under the above described process. The next and last process in the preparation of bacon and hams, previous to being sent to market, is drying. This is effected by hanging the flitches and hams for 2 or 3 weeks in a room heated by stoves, or in a smoke-house, in which they are exposed for the same length of time to the smoke arising from the slow combustion of the sawdust of oak or other hard wood. The latter mode of completing the curing process has some advantages over the other, as by it the meat is subject to the action of *creosote*, a volatile oil produced by the combustion of the sawdust, which is powerfully antiseptic. The process also furnishing a thin covering of a resinous varnish, excludes the air not only from the muscle, but also from the fat—thus effectually preventing the meat from becoming rusted; and the principal reasons for condemning the practice of removing the ribs from the flitches of pork are, that by so doing the meat becomes unpleasantly hard and pungent in the process of salting, and, by being more exposed to the action of the air, becomes sooner and more extensively rusted. Notwithstanding its superior efficacy in completing the process of curing, the flavour which smoke-drying imparts to meat is disliked by many persons, and it is therefore by no means the most general mode of drying adopted by mercantile curers. A very impure variety of *pyroligneous* acid, or vinegar made from the destructive distillation of wood, is sometimes used, on account of the highly preservative power of the creosote which it contains, and also to impart the smoke-flavour; in which latter object, however, the coarse flavour of tar is given, rather than that derived from the smoke from combustion of wood. A considerable portion of the bacon and hams salted in Ireland is exported from that country packed amongst salt, in bales, immediately from the salting process, without having been in any degree dried. In the process of salting above described, pork loses from 8 to 10 per cent of its weight, according to the size and quality of the meat; and a further diminution of weight, to the extent of 5 to 6 per cent. takes place in drying during the first fortnight after being taken out of salt; so that the total loss in weight occasioned by the preparation of bacon and hams in a proper state for market, is not less on an average than 15 per cent. on the weight of the fresh pork.

BACON, to Cure and Keep it free from Rust (Cobbett's Recipe).

The two sides that remain, and which are called flitches, are to be cured for bacon. They are first rubbed with salt on their insides, or flesh sides, then placed one on the other, the flesh sides uppermost, in a salting-trough which has a gutter round its edges to drain away the brine; for, to have sweet and fine bacon, the flitches must not be sopping in brine, which gives it the sort of vile taste that barrel and sea pork have. Every one knows how different is the taste of fresh dry salt from that of salt in a dissolved state; therefore change the salt often,—once in 4 or 5 days; let it melt and sink in, but not lie too long; twice change the flitches, put that at bottom which was first on the top: this mode will cost you a great deal more in salt than the sopping mode, but without it your bacon will not be so sweet and fine, nor keep so well. As for the time required in making your flitches sufficiently salt, it depends on circumstances. It takes a longer time for a thick than a thin flitch, and longer in dry than in damp weather, or in a dry than in a damp place; but for the flitches of a hog of five score, in weather not very dry or damp, about 6 weeks may do; and as yours is to be fat, which receives little injury from over-salting, give time enough, for you are to have bacon until Christmas comes again. The place for salting should, like a dairy, always be cool, but well ventilated; confined air, though cool, will taint meat sooner than the midday sun accompanied by a breeze. With regard to smoking the bacon, two precautions are necessary: first, to hang the flitches where no rain comes down upon them; and next, that the smoke must proceed from wood, not peat, turf, or coal. As to the time required to smoke a flitch, it depends a good deal upon whether there be a constant fire beneath; and whether the fire be large or small: a month will do, if the fire be pretty constant and rich, as a farm-house fire usually is; but over-smoking, or rather too long hanging in the air, makes the bacon rust; great attention should therefore be paid to this matter. The flitch ought not to be dried up to the hardness of a board, and yet it ought to be perfectly dry. Before you hang it up, lay it on the floor, scatter the flesh side pretty thickly over with bran, or with some fine sawdust, not of deal or fir; rub it on the flesh, or pat it well down upon it: this keeps the smoke from getting into the little openings, and makes a sort of crust to be dried on. To keep the bacon sweet and good, and free from hoppers, sift fine some clean and dry wood ashes. Put some at the bottom of a box or chest long enough to hold a flitch of bacon; lay in one flitch, then put in more ashes, then another flitch, and cover this with six or eight inches of the ashes. The place where the box or chest is kept ought to be dry, and, should the ashes become damp, they should be put in the fireplace to dry, and when cold, put back again. With these precautions, the bacon will be as good at the end of the year as on the first day. For simple general rules, these may be safely taken as a guide; and those who implicitly follow the directions given, will possess at the expiration of from 6 weeks to 2 months well-flavoured and well-cured bacon.

BACON or HAMS, to Cure in the Devonshire way.

Ingredients.—To every 14 lbs. of meat allow 2 oz. of saltpetre, 2 oz. of salt prunella, 1 lb. of common salt. For the pickle, 3 gallons of water, 5 lbs. of common salt, 7 lbs. of coarse sugar, 3 lbs. of bay salt. *Mode.*—Weigh the sides, hams, and cheeks, and to every 14 lbs. allow the above proportion of saltpetre, salt prunella, and common salt. Pound and mix these together, and rub well into the meat; lay it in a stone trough or tub, rubbing it thoroughly, and turning it daily for two successive days. At the end of the second day, pour on it a pickle made as follows:—Put the above ingredients into a saucepan, set it on the fire, and stir frequently; remove all the scum, allow it to boil for ¼ hour, and pour it hot over the meat. Let the hams, &c., be well rubbed and turned daily; if the meat is small, a fortnight will be sufficient for the sides and shoulders to remain in the pickle, and the hams 3 weeks; if from 30 lbs. and upwards, 3 weeks will be required for the sides, &c., and from 4 to 5 weeks for the hams. On taking the pieces out, let them drain for an hour, cover with dry sawdust, and smoke from a fortnight to three weeks. Boil and carefully skim the pickle after using, and it will keep good, closely corked, for 2 years. When boiling it for use, add about 2 lbs. of common salt, and the same of treacle, to allow for waste. Tongues are excellent put into this pickle cold, having been first rubbed well with saltpetre and salt, and allowed to remain 24 hours, not forgetting to make a deep incision under the thick part of the tongue, so as to allow the pickle to penetrate more readily. A fortnight or three weeks, according to the size of the tongue, will be sufficient. *Time.*—Small meat to remain in the pickle a fortnight, hams 3 weeks; to be smoked from a fortnight to 3 weeks.

BACON, to Cure in the Wiltshire way.

Ingredients.—1½ lb. of coarse sugar, ½ lb. of bay salt, 6 oz. of saltpetre, 1 lb. of common salt. *Mode.*—Sprinkle each flitch with salt, and let the blood drain off for 24 hours; then pound and mix the above ingredients well together and rub it well into the meat, which should be turned every day for a month; then hang it to dry, and afterwards smoke it for 10 days. *Time.*—To remain in the pickle from three to four weeks, to be smoked 10 days, or rather longer.

BACON, Fried Rashers of, and Poached Eggs.

Ingredients.—Bacon; eggs. *Mode.*—Cut the bacon into thin slices, trim away the rusty parts, and cut off the rind. Put it into a *cold* frying-pan, that is to say, do not place the pan on the fire before the bacon is in it. Turn it 2 or 3 times, and dish it on a very hot dish. Poach the eggs and slip them on to the bacon without breaking the yolks, and serve quickly. *Time.*—3 or 4 minutes. *Average cost*, 10*d.* to 1*s.* per lb. for the primest parts. *Sufficient.*—Allow 6 eggs for 3 persons. *Seasonable* at any time. *Note.*—Fried rashers of bacon, curled, serve as a pretty garnish to many dishes; and, for small families, answer very well as a substitute for boiled bacon, to serve with a small dish of poultry, &c.

The Bain Marie.—It is an open kind of vessel, as shown in the engraving, and is a utensil much used in modern cookery, both in English and French kitchens. It is filled with boiling or nearly boiling water; and into this water should be put all the stewpans containing those ingredients which it is desired to keep hot. The quantity and quality of the contents of these vessels are not at all affected; and if the hour of dinner is uncertain in any establishment, by reason of the nature of the master's business, nothing is so sure a means of preserving the flavour of all dishes as the employment of the bain marie.

THE BAIN MARIE.

BARBEL.

Ingredients.—½ pint of port wine, a saltspoonful of salt, 2 tablespoonfuls of vinegar, 2 sliced onions, a faggot of sweet herbs, nutmeg and mace to taste, the juice of a lemon, 2 anchovies; 1 or 2 barbels, according to size. *Mode.*—Boil the barbels in salt and water till done; pour off some of the water, and to the remainder put the ingredients mentioned above. Simmer gently for ½ hour or rather more, and strain. Put in the fish, heat it gradually, but do not let it boil, or it will be broken. *Time.*—Altogether 1 hour. *Sufficient* for 4 persons. *Seasonable* from September to November.

BARBERRIES (Berberis vulgaris).

A fruit of such great acidity, that even birds refuse to eat it. In this respect, it nearly approaches the tamarind. When boiled with sugar, it makes a very agreeable preserve or jelly, according to the different modes of preparing it. Barberries are also used as a dry sweetmeat, and in sugarplums or comfits; are pickled with vinegar, and are used for various culinary purposes. They are well calculated to allay heat and thirst in persons afflicted with fevers. The berries, arranged on bunches of nicely curled parsley, make an exceedingly pretty garnish for supper dishes, particularly for white meats, like boiled fowl à la Béchamel, the three colours, scarlet, green, and white, contrasting well, and producing a very good effect.

BARBERRIES, to preserve in Bunches.

Ingredients.—1 pint of syrup, barberries. *Mode.*—Prepare some small pieces of clean white wood, 3 inches long and ¼ inch wide, and tie the fruit on to these in nice bunches. Have ready some clear syrup (*see* Syrup); put in the barberries, and simmer them in it for 2 successive days, boiling them for nearly ½ hour each day, and covering them each time with the syrup when cold. When the fruit looks perfectly clear it is sufficiently done, and should be stowed away in pots, with the syrup poured over, or the fruit may be candied. *Time.*—½ hour to simmer each day. *Seasonable* in autumn.

BARLEY SOUP.

Ingredients.—2 lbs. of shin of beef, ¼ lb. of pearl barley, a large bunch of parsley, 4 onions, 6 potatoes, salt and pepper, 4 quarts of water. *Mode.*—Put in all the ingredients, and simmer gently for 3 hours. *Time.*—3 hours. *Average cost*, 2½d. per quart. *Seasonable* all the year, but more suitable for winter.

BARLEY-SUGAR, to make.

Ingredients.—To every lb. of sugar allow ½ pint of water, ½ the white of an egg. *Mode.*—Put the sugar into a well-tinned saucepan, with the water, and, when the former is dissolved, set it over a moderate fire, adding the well-beaten egg before the mixture gets warm, and stir it well together. When it boils, remove the scum as it rises, and keep it boiling until no more appears, and the syrup looks perfectly clear; then strain it through a fine sieve or muslin bag, and put it back into the saucepan. Boil it again like caramel, until it is brittle, when a little is dropped in a basin of cold water: it is then sufficiently boiled. Add a little lemon-juice and a few drops of essence of lemon, and let it stand for a minute or two. Have ready a marble slab or large dish, rubbed over with salad-oil; pour on it the sugar, and cut it into strips with a pair of scissors: these strips should then be twisted, and the barley-sugar stored away in a very dry place. It may be formed into lozenges or drops, by dropping the sugar in a very small quantity at a time on to the oiled slab or dish. *Time.*—¼ hour. *Average cost*, 7d. *Sufficient* for 5 or 6 sticks.

BARLEY-WATER, to make.

Ingredients.—2 oz. of pearl barley, 2 quarts of boiling water, 1 pint of cold water. *Mode.*—Wash the barley in cold water; put it into a saucepan with the above proportion of cold water, and when it has boiled for about ¼ hour, strain off the water, and add the 2 quarts of fresh boiling water. Boil it until the liquid is reduced one half; strain it, and it will be ready for use. It may be flavoured with lemon-peel, after being sweetened, or a small piece may be simmered with the barley. When the invalid may take it, a little lemon-juice gives this pleasant drink in illness a very nice flavour; as does also a small quantity of port wine. *Time.*—To boil until the liquid is reduced one half. *Sufficient* to make 1 quart of barley-water.

BATTER PUDDING, Baked.

Ingredients.—1½ pint of milk, 4 tablespoonfuls of flour, 2 oz. of butter, 4 eggs, a little salt. *Mode.*—Mix the flour with a small quantity of cold milk; make the remainder hot, and pour it on to the flour, keeping the mixture well stirred; add the butter, eggs, and salt; beat the whole well, and put the pudding into a buttered pie-dish; bake for ¾ hour, and serve with sweet sauce, wine sauce, or stewed fruit. Baked in small cups, very pretty little puddings may be made; they should be eaten with the same accompaniments as above. *Time.*—¾ hour. *Average cost,* 9d. *Sufficient* for 5 or 6 persons. *Seasonable* at any time.

BATTER PUDDING, Baked, with Dried or Fresh Fruit.

Ingredients.—1½ pint of milk, 4 tablespoonfuls of flour, 3 eggs, 2 oz. of finely-shredded suet, ¼ lb. of currants, a pinch of salt. *Mode.*—Mix the milk, flour, and eggs to a smooth batter; add a little salt, the suet, and the currants, which should be well washed, picked, and dried; put the mixture into a buttered pie-dish, and bake in a moderate oven for 1¼ hour. When fresh fruits are in season, this pudding is exceedingly nice, with damsons, plums, red currants, gooseberries, or apples; when made with these, the pudding must be thickly sprinkled over with sifted sugar. Boiled batter pudding, with fruit, is made in the same manner, by putting the fruit into a buttered basin, and filling it up with batter made in the above proportion, but omitting the suet. It must be sent quickly to table, and covered plentifully with sifted sugar. *Time.*—Baked batter pudding, with fruit, 1¼ to 1½ hour; boiled ditto, 1½ to 1¾ hour, allowing that both are made with the above proportion of batter. Smaller puddings will be done enough in ¾ or 1 hour. *Average cost,* 10*d. Sufficient* for 7 or 8 persons. *Seasonable* at any time, with dried fruits.

BATTER PUDDING, Boiled.

Ingredients.—3 eggs, 1 oz. of butter, 1 pint of milk, 3 tablespoonfuls of flour, a little salt. *Mode.*—Put the flour into a basin, and add sufficient milk to moisten it; carefully rub down all the lumps with a spoon, then pour in the remainder of the milk, and stir in the butter, which should be previously melted; keep beating the mixture, add the eggs and a pinch of salt, and, when the batter is quite smooth, put it into a well-buttered basin, tie it down very tightly, and put it into boiling water; move the basin about for a few minutes after it is put into the water, to prevent the flour settling in any part, and boil for 1¼ hour. This pudding may also be boiled in a floured cloth that has been wetted in hot water: it will then take a few minutes less than when boiled in a basin. Send batter puddings very quickly to table, and serve with sweet sauce, wine sauce, stewed fruit, or jam of any kind: when the latter is used, a little of it may be placed round the dish in small quantities, as a garnish. *Time.*—1¼ hour in a basin, 1 hour in a cloth. *Average cost,* 7*d. Sufficient* for 5 or 6 persons. *Seasonable* at any time.

BATTER PUDDING, with Orange Marmalade.

Ingredients.—4 eggs, 1 pint of milk, 1½ oz. of loaf sugar, 3 tablespoonfuls of flour. *Mode.*—Make the batter with the above ingredients, put it into a well-buttered basin, tie it down with a cloth, and boil for 1 hour. As soon as it is turned out of the basin, put a small jar of orange marmalade all over the top, and send the pudding very quickly to table. It is advisable to warm the marmalade to make it liquid. *Time.*—1 hour. *Average cost,* with the marmalade, 1*s.* 3*d. Sufficient* for 5 or 6 persons. *Seasonable* at any time; but more suitable for a winter pudding.

BEANS, Boiled Broad or Windsor.

BROAD BEANS.

Ingredients.—To each ½ gallon of water, allow 1 heaped tablespoonful of salt; beans. *Mode.*—This is a favourite vegetable with many persons, but, to be nice, should be young and freshly gathered. After shelling the beans, put them into *boiling* water, salted in the above proportion, and let them boil rapidly until tender. Drain them well in a colander; dish, and serve with them separately a tureen of parsley and butter. Boiled bacon should always accompany this vegetable, but the beans should be cooked separately. It is usually served with the beans laid round, and the parsley and butter in a tureen. Beans also make an excellent garnish to a ham, and when used for this purpose, if very old, should have their skins removed. *Time.*—Very young beans, 15 minutes; when a moderate size, 20 to 25 minutes, or longer. *Average cost*, unshelled, 6*d.* per peck. *Sufficient.*—Allow one peck for 6 or 7 persons. *Seasonable* in July and August.

BEANS, Broad, à la Poulette.

Ingredients.—2 pints of broad beans, ½ pint of stock or broth, a small bunch of savoury herbs, including parsley, a small lump of sugar, the yolk of 1 egg, ¼ pint of cream, pepper and salt to taste. *Mode.*—Procure some young and freshly-gathered beans, and shell sufficient to make 2 pints; boil them, as in the preceding recipe, until nearly done; then drain them and put them into a stewpan with the stock, finely-minced herbs, and sugar. Stew the beans until perfectly tender, and the liquor has dried away a little; then beat up the yolk of an egg with the cream, add this to the beans, let the whole get thoroughly hot, and when on the point of simmering, serve. Should the beans be very large, the skin should be removed previously to boiling them. *Time.*—10 minutes to boil the beans, 15 minutes to stew them in the stock. *Average cost*, unshelled, 6*d.* per peck. *Seasonable* in July and August.

BEANS, Boiled French.

Ingredients.—To each ½ gallon of water allow 1 heaped tablespoonful of salt, a very small piece of soda. *Mode.*—This vegetable should always be eaten young, as when allowed to grow too long it tastes stringy and tough when cooked. Cut off the heads and tails, and a thin strip on each side of the beans to remove the strings; then divide each bean into 4 or 6 pieces, according to size, cutting them lengthways in a slanting direction, and as they are cut put them into cold water, with a small quantity of salt dissolved in it. Have ready a saucepan of boiling water, with salt and soda in the above proportion; put in the beans, keep them boiling quickly, with the lid uncovered, and be careful that they do not get smoked. When tender, which may be ascertained by their sinking to the bottom of the saucepan, take them up, pour them into a colander, and when drained, dish and serve with plain melted butter. When very young, beans are sometimes served whole: thus dressed, their colour and flavour are much better preserved, but the more general way of sending them to table is to cut them into thin strips. *Time.*—Very young beans, 10 to 12 minutes; moderate size, 15 to 20 minutes, after the water boils. *Average cost*, in full season, 1*s.* 4*d.* per peck, but when forced very expensive. *Sufficient.*—Allow ½ peck for 6 or 7 persons. *Seasonable* from the middle of July to the end of September, but may be had forced from February to the beginning of June.

BEANS, French Mode of Cooking French.

Ingredients.—A quart of French beans, 3 oz. of fresh butter, pepper and salt to taste, the juice of ½ lemon. *Mode.*—Cut and boil the beans by the preceding recipe, and when tender, put them into a stewpan, and shake over the fire, to dry away the moisture from the beans. When quite dry and hot, add the butter, pepper, salt, and lemon-juice; keep moving the stewpan, without using a spoon, as that would break the beans; and when the butter is melted, and all is thoroughly hot, serve. If the butter should not mix well, add a tablespoonful of gravy, and serve very quickly. *Time.*—About ¼ hour to boil the beans; 10 minutes to shake them over the fire. *Average cost*, in full season, about 1*s.* 4*d.* per peck. *Sufficient* for 3 or 4 persons. *Seasonable* from the middle of July to the end of September.

BEANS, to Boil Haricots Blancs, or White Haricot.

Ingredients.—1 quart of white haricot beans, 2 quarts of soft water, 1 oz. of butter, 1 heaped tablespoonful of salt. *Mode.*—Put the beans into cold water, let them soak from 2 to 4 hours, according to their age; then put them into cold water salted in the above proportion, bring them to boil, and let them simmer very slowly until tender; pour the water away from them, let them stand by the side of the fire, with the lid of the saucepan partially off, to allow the beans to dry; then add 1 oz. of butter and a seasoning of pepper and salt. Shake the beans about for a minute or two, and serve: do not stir them with a spoon, for fear of breaking them to pieces. *Time.*—After the water boils, from 2 to 2½ hours. *Average cost,* 4*d.* per quart. *Sufficient* for 4 or 5 persons. *Seasonable* in winter, when other vegetables are scarce.

Note.—Haricots blancs, when new and fresh, should be put into boiling water, and do not require any soaking previous to dressing.

BEANS, Haricots Blancs & Minced Onions.

Ingredients.—1 quart of white haricot beans, 4 middling-sized onions, ¼ pint of good brown gravy, pepper and salt to taste, a little flour. *Mode.*—Peel and mince the onions not too finely, and fry them in butter of a light brown colour; dredge over them a little flour, and add the gravy and a seasoning of pepper and salt. Have ready a pint of haricot beans well boiled and drained; put them with the onions and gravy, mix all well together, and serve very hot. *Time.*—From 2 to 2½ hours to boil the beans; 5 minutes to fry the onions. *Average cost,* 4*d.* per quart. *Sufficient* for 4 or 5 persons. *Seasonable* in winter.

BEANS, Haricots Blancs à la Maître d'Hôtel.

HARICOT BEANS.

Ingredients.—1 quart of white haricot beans, ¼ lb. of fresh butter, 1 tablespoonful of minced parsley, pepper and salt to taste, the juice of ½ lemon. *Mode.*—Should the beans be very dry, soak them for an hour or two in cold water, and boil them until perfectly tender, as in the preceding recipe. If the water should boil away, replenish it with a little more cold, which makes the skin of the beans tender. Let them be very thoroughly done; drain them well; then add to them the butter, minced parsley, and a seasoning of pepper and salt. Keep moving the stewpan over the fire without using a spoon, as this would break the beans; and, when the various ingredients are well mixed with them, squeeze in the lemon-juice, and serve very hot. *Time.*—From 2 to 2½ hours to boil the beans. *Average cost*, 4*d.* per quart. *Sufficient* for 4 or 5 persons. *Seasonable* in winter.

BÉCHAMEL, or French White Sauce.

Ingredients.—1 small bunch of parsley, 2 cloves, ½ bay-leaf, 1 small bunch of savoury herbs, salt to taste; 3 or 4 mushrooms, when obtainable; 2 pints of white stock, 1 pint of milk or cream, 1 tablespoonful of arrowroot. *Mode.*—Put the stock into a stewpan, with the parsley, cloves, bay-leaf, herbs, and mushrooms; add a seasoning of salt, but no pepper, as that would give the sauce a dusty appearance, and should be avoided. When it has boiled long enough to extract the flavour of the herbs, &c., strain it, and boil it up quickly again, until it is nearly half reduced. Now mix the arrowroot smoothly with the milk or cream, and let it simmer very gently for 5 minutes over a slow fire; pour to it the stock, and continue to simmer slowly for 10 minutes, if the sauce be thick. If, on the contrary, it be too thin, it must be stirred over a sharp fire till it thickens. Always make it thick, as it can easily be thinned with cream, milk, or white stock. This sauce is excellent for pouring over boiled fowls. *Time.*—Altogether, 2 hours. *Average cost*, 3*s.* per quart, with cream at 1*s.* 6*d.* per pint.

BÉCHAMEL MAIGRE, or Without Meat.

Ingredients.—2 onions, 1 blade of mace, mushroom trimmings, a small bunch of parsley, 1 oz. of butter, flour, ½ pint of water, 1 pint of milk, salt, the juice of ½ lemon, 2 eggs. *Mode.*—Put in a stewpan the milk and ½ pint of water, with the onions, mace, mushrooms, parsley, and salt. Let these simmer gently for 20 minutes. In the meantime, rub on a plate 1 oz. of flour and butter; put it to the liquor, and stir it well till it boils up; then place it by the side of the fire, and continue stirring until it is perfectly smooth. Now strain it through a sieve into a basin, after which put it back in the stewpan, and add the lemon-juice. Beat up the yolks of the eggs with about 4 dessertspoonfuls of milk; strain this to the sauce, keep stirring it over the fire, *but do not let it boil, or it will curdle. Time.*—Altogether, ¾ hour. *Average cost*, 5*d.* per pint.

This is a good sauce to pour over boiled fowls when they are a bad colour.

BEEF, Aitchbone of, Boiled.

Ingredients.—Beef, water. *Mode.*—After this joint has been in salt 5 or 6 days, it will be ready for use, and will not take so long boiling as a round, for it is not so solid. Wash the meat, and, if too salt, soak it for a few hours, changing the water once or twice, till the required freshness is obtained. Put into a saucepan, or boiling-pot, sufficient water to cover the meat; set it over the fire, and when it boils, plunge in the joint, and let it boil up quickly. Now draw the pot to the side of the fire, and let the process be very gradual, as the water must only simmer, or the meat will be hard and tough. Carefully remove the scum from the surface of the water, and continue doing this for a few minutes after it first boils. Carrots and turnips are served with this dish, and sometimes suet dumplings, which may be boiled with the beef. Garnish with a few of the carrots and turnips, and serve the remainder in a vegetable-dish. *Time.*—An aitchbone of 10 lbs., 2½ hours after the water boils; one of 20 lbs., 4 hours. *Average cost*, 6*d.* per lb. *Sufficient.*—10 lbs. for 7 or 8 persons. *Seasonable* all the year, but best from September to March.

AITCH-BONE OF BEEF.

Note.—The liquor in which the meat has been boiled may be easily converted into a very excellent pea-soup. It will require very few vegetables, as it will be impregnated with the flavour of those boiled with the meat.

BEEF À LA MODE.

Ingredients.—6 or 7 lbs. of the thick flank of beef, a few slices of fat bacon, 1 teacupful of vinegar, black pepper, allspice, 2 cloves well mixed and finely pounded, making altogether 1 heaped teaspoonful; salt to taste, 1 bunch of savoury herbs, including parsley, all finely minced and well mixed; 3 onions, 2 large carrots, 1 turnip, 1 head of celery, 1½ pint of water, 1 glass of port wine. *Mode.*—Slice and fry the onions of a pale brown, and cut up the other vegetables in small pieces, and prepare the beef for stewing in the following manner:—Choose a fine piece of beef, cut the bacon into long slices, about an inch in thickness, dip them into vinegar, and then into a little of the above seasoning of spice, &c., mixed with the same quantity of minced herbs. With a sharp knife make holes deep enough to let in the bacon; then rub the beef over with the remainder of the seasoning and herbs, and bind it up in a nice shape with tape. Have ready a well-tinned stewpan (it should not be much larger than the piece of meat you are cooking), into which put the beef, with the vegetables, vinegar, and water. Let it simmer *very gently* for 5 hours, or rather longer, should the meat not be extremely tender, and turn it once or twice. When ready to serve, take out the beef, remove the tape, and put it on a hot dish. Skim off every particle of fat from the gravy, add the port wine, just let it boil, pour it over the beef, and it is ready to serve. Great care must be taken that this does not boil fast, or the meat will be tough and tasteless; it should only just bubble. When convenient, all kinds of stews, &c. should be cooked on a hot plate, as the process is so much more gradual than on an open fire. *Time.*—5 hours, or rather more. *Average cost,* 7*d.* per lb. *Sufficient* for 7 or 8 persons. *Seasonable* all the year, but more suitable for a winter dish.

BEEF À LA MODE (Economical).

Ingredients.—About 3 lbs. of clod or sticking of beef, 2 oz. of clarified dripping, 1 large onion, flour, 2 quarts of water, 12 berries of allspice, 2 bay-leaves, ½ teaspoonful of whole black pepper, salt to taste. *Mode.*—Cut the beef into small pieces, and roll them in flour; put the dripping into a stewpan with the onion, which should be sliced thin. Let it get quite hot; lay in the pieces of beef, and stir them well about. When nicely browned all over, add *by degrees* boiling water in the above proportion, and, as the water is added, keep the whole well stirred. Put in the spice, bay-leaves, and seasoning, cover the stewpan closely, and set it by the side of the fire to stew very *gently,* till the meat becomes quite tender, which will be in about 3 hours, when it will be ready to serve. Remove the bay-leaves before it is sent to table. *Time.*—3 hours. *Average cost,* 1*s.* 3*d. Sufficient* for 6 persons. *Seasonable* at any time.

BEEF, Baked.

[Cold Meat Cookery. 1.] *Ingredients.*—About 2 lbs. of cold roast beef, 2 small onions, 1 large carrot or 2 small ones, 1 turnip, a small bunch of savoury herbs, salt and pepper to taste, quite ½ pint of gravy, 3 tablespoonfuls of ale, crust or mashed potatoes. *Mode.*—Cut the beef in slices, allowing a small amount of fat to each slice; place a layer of this in the bottom of a pie-dish, with a portion of the onions, carrots, and turnips, which must be sliced; mince the herbs, strew them over the meat, and season with pepper and salt. Then put another layer of meat, vegetables, and seasoning; and proceed in this manner until all the ingredients are used. Pour in the gravy and ale (water may be substituted for the former, but it is not so nice), cover with a crust or mashed potatoes, and bake for ½ hour, or rather longer. *Time.*—Rather more than ½ hour. *Average cost,* exclusive of the meat, 6*d*. *Sufficient* for 5 or 6 persons. *Seasonable* at any time.

Note.—It is as well to parboil the carrots and turnips before adding them to the meat, and to use some of the liquor in which they were boiled as a substitute for gravy; that is to say, when there is no gravy at hand. Be particular to cut the onions in very *thin* slices.

[COLD MEAT COOKERY. 2.] *Ingredients.*—Slices of cold roast beef, salt and pepper to taste, 1 sliced onion, 1 teaspoonful of minced savoury herbs, 12 tablespoonfuls of gravy or sauce of any kind, mashed potatoes. *Mode.*—Butter the sides of a deep dish, and spread mashed potatoes over the bottom of it; on this place layers of beef in thin slices (this may be minced, if there is not sufficient beef to cut into slices), well seasoned with pepper and salt, and a very little onion and herbs, which should be previously fried of a nice brown; then put another layer of mashed potatoes, and beef, and other ingredients, as before; pour in the gravy or sauce, cover the whole with another layer of potatoes, and bake for ½ hour. This may be served in the dish, or turned out. *Time.*—½ hour. *Average cost,* exclusive of the cold beef, 6*d*. *Sufficient.*—A large pie-dish full for 5 or 6 persons. *Seasonable* at any time.

BEEF-BONES, Broiled.

[COLD MEAT COOKERY.] *Ingredients.*—The bones of ribs or sirloin; salt, pepper and cayenne. *Mode.*—Separate the bones, taking care that the meat on them is not too thick in any part; sprinkle them well with the above seasoning, and broil over a very clear fire. When nicely browned, they are done; but do not allow them to blacken.

BEEF, Brisket of, à la Flamande.

Ingredients.—About 6 or 8 lbs. of the brisket of beef, 4 or 5 slices of bacon, 2 carrots, 1 onion, a bunch of savoury herbs, salt and pepper to taste, 4 cloves, 4 whole allspice, 2 blades of mace. *Mode.*—Choose that portion of the brisket which contains the gristle, trim it, and put it into a stewpan with the slices of bacon, which should be placed under and over the meat. Add the vegetables, herbs, spices, and seasoning, and cover with a little weak stock or water; shut the stewpan-lid as closely as possible, and simmer very gently for 4 hours. Strain the liquor, reserve a portion of it for sauce, and the remainder boil quickly over a sharp fire until reduced to a glaze, with which glaze the meat. Garnish the dish with scooped carrots and turnips, and, when liked, a little cabbage; all of which must be cooked separately. Thicken and flavour the liquor that was saved for sauce, pour it round the meat, and serve. The beef may also be garnished with glazed onions, artichoke-bottoms, &c. *Time.*—4 hours. *Average cost*, 7d. per lb. *Sufficient* for 6 or 8 persons. *Seasonable* at any time.

BEEF, Brisket of, Stewed.

Ingredients.—7 lbs. of the brisket of beef, vinegar and salt, 6 carrots, 6 turnips, 6 small onions, 1 blade of pounded mace, 2 whole allspice pounded, thickening of butter and flour, 2 tablespoonfuls of ketchup; stock, or water. *Mode.*—About an hour before dressing it, rub the meat over with vinegar and salt; put it into a stewpan, with sufficient stock to cover it (when this is not at hand, water may be substituted for it), and be particular that the stewpan is not much larger than the meat. Skim well, and when it has simmered very gently for 1 hour, put in the vegetables, and continue simmering till the meat is perfectly tender. Draw out the bones, dish the meat, and garnish either with tufts of cauliflower or braised cabbage cut in quarters. Thicken as much gravy as required, with a little butter and flour; add spices and ketchup in the above proportion, give one boil, pour some of it over the meat, and the remainder send in a tureen. *Time.*—Rather more than 3 hours. *Average cost*, 7d. per lb. *Sufficient* for 7 or 8 persons. *Seasonable* at any time.

Note.—The remainder of the liquor in which the beef was boiled may be served as a soup, or it may be sent to table with the meat in a tureen.

BEEF, Broiled, and Mushroom Sauce.

[Cold Meat Cookery.] *Ingredients*.—2 or 3 dozen small button mushrooms, 1 oz. of butter, salt and cayenne to taste, 1 tablespoonful of mushroom ketchup, mashed potatoes, slices of cold roast beef. *Mode*.—Wipe the mushrooms free from grit with a piece of flannel, and salt; put them in a stewpan with the butter, seasoning, and ketchup; stir over the fire until the mushrooms are quite done, when pour it in the middle of mashed potatoes, browned. Then place round the potatoes slices of cold roast beef, nicely broiled over a clear fire. In making the mushroom sauce the ketchup may be dispensed with, if there is sufficient gravy. *Time*.—¼ hour. *Average cost*, exclusive of the meat, 8*d*. *Seasonable* from August to October.

BEEF, Broiled, and Oyster Sauce.

[Cold Meat Cookery.] *Ingredients*.—2 dozen oysters, 3 cloves, 1 blade of mace, 2 oz. of butter, ½ teaspoonful of flour, cayenne and salt to taste, mashed potatoes, a few slices of cold roast beef. *Mode*.—Put the oysters in a stewpan, with their liquor strained; add the cloves, mace, butter, flour, and seasoning, and let them simmer gently for 5 minutes. Have ready in the centre of a dish round walls of mashed potatoes, browned; into the middle pour the oyster sauce quite hot, and round the potatoes place, in layers, slices of the beef, which should be previously broiled over a nice clear fire. *Time*.—5 minutes. *Average cost*, 1*s*. 6*d*., exclusive of the cold meat. *Sufficient* for 4 or 5 persons. *Seasonable* from September to April.

BEEF BUBBLE-AND-SQUEAK.

[Cold Meat Cookery.] *Ingredients*.—A few thin slices of cold boiled beef; butter, cabbage, 1 sliced onion, pepper and salt to taste. *Mode*.—Fry the slices of beef gently in a little butter, taking care not to dry them up. Lay them on a flat dish, and cover with fried greens. The greens may be prepared from cabbage sprouts or green savoys. They should be boiled till tender, well drained, minced, and placed till quite hot in a frying-pan, with butter, a sliced onion, and seasoning of pepper and salt. When the onion is done it is ready to serve. *Time*.—Altogether, ½ hour. *Average cost*, exclusive of the cold beef, 3*d*. *Seasonable* at any time.

BEEF CAKE.

[COLD MEAT COOKERY.] *Ingredients.*—The remains of cold roast beef; to each pound of cold meat allow ¼ lb. of bacon or ham; seasoning to taste of pepper and salt, 1 small bunch of minced savoury herbs, 1 or 2 eggs. *Mode.*—Mince the beef very finely (if underdone it will be better), add to it the bacon, which must also be chopped very small, and mix well together. Season, stir in the herbs, and bind with an egg, or 2 should 1 not be sufficient. Make it into small square cakes, about ½ inch thick, fry them in hot dripping, drain them, and serve in a dish with good gravy poured round. *Time.*—10 minutes. *Average cost*, exclusive of the cold meat, 6*d*. *Seasonable* at any time.

BEEF, Collared.

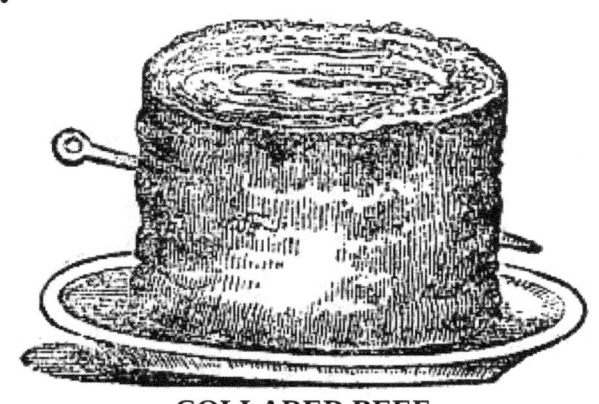

COLLARED BEEF.

Ingredients.—7 lbs. of the thin end of the flank of beef, 2 oz. of coarse sugar, 6 oz. of salt, 1 oz. of saltpetre, 1 large handful of parsley, minced, 1 dessertspoonful of minced sage, a bunch of savoury herbs, ½ teaspoonful of pounded allspice; salt and pepper to taste. *Mode.*—Choose fine tender beef, but not too fat; lay it in a dish, rub in the sugar, salt, and saltpetre, and let it remain in the pickle for a week or ten days, turning and rubbing it every day. Then bone it, remove all the gristle and the coarse skin of the inside part, and sprinkle it thickly with parsley, herbs, spice, and seasoning in the above proportion, taking care that the former are finely minced, and the latter well pounded. Roll the meat up in a cloth as tightly as possible; bind it firmly with broad tape, and boil it gently for 6 hours. Immediately on taking it out of the pot put it under a good weight, without undoing it, and let it remain until cold. This dish is a very nice addition to the breakfast-table. *Time.*—6 hours. *Average cost*, for this quantity, 4s. *Seasonable* at any time.

Note.—During the time the beef is in pickle it should be kept cool, and regularly rubbed and turned every day.

BEEF COLLOPS.

Ingredients.—2 lbs. of rump-steak, ¼ lb. of butter, 1 pint of gravy (water may be substituted for this), salt and pepper to taste, 1 shalot, finely minced, ½ pickled walnut, 1 teaspoonful of capers. *Mode.*—Have the steak cut thin, and divide it in pieces about 3 inches long; beat these with the blade of a knife, and dredge with flour. Put them in a frying-pan with the butter, and let them fry for about 3 minutes; then lay them in a small stewpan, and pour over them the gravy. Add a piece of butter kneaded with a little flour, put in the seasoning and all the other ingredients, and let the whole simmer, but not boil, for 10 minutes. Serve in a hot covered dish. *Time.*—10 minutes. *Average cost*, 1s. per lb. *Sufficient* for 4 or 5 persons. *Seasonable* at any time.

BEEF CARVING.

Beef, Aitchbone of.—A boiled aitchbone of beef is not a difficult joint to carve, as will be seen on reference to the accompanying engraving. By following with the knife the direction of the line from 1 to 2, nice slices will be easily cut. It may be necessary, as in a round of beef, to cut a thick slice off the outside before commencing to serve.

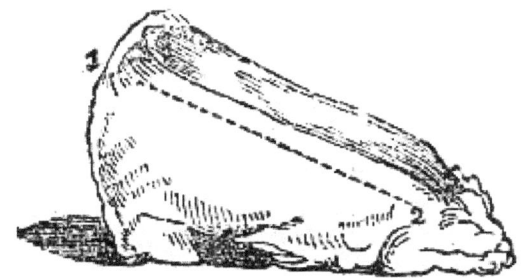

Beef, Brisket of.—There is but little description necessary to add to show the carving of a boiled brisket of beef beyond the engraving here inserted. The only point to be observed is, that the joint should be cut evenly and firmly quite across the bones, so that on its reappearance at table it should not have a jagged and untidy look.

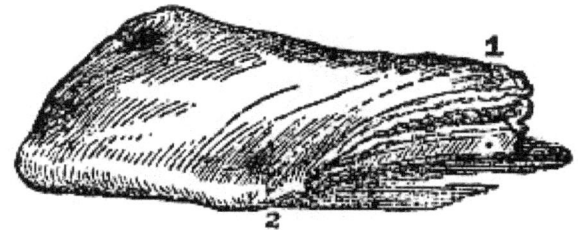

Beef, Ribs of.—This dish resembles the sirloin, except that it has no fillet or undercut. As explained in the recipes, the end piece is often cut off, salted and boiled. The mode of carving is similar to that of the sirloin, viz., in the direction of the dotted line from 1 to 2. This joint will be the more easily cut if the plan be pursued which is suggested in carving the sirloin; namely, the inserting of the knife immediately between the bone and the meat, before commencing to cut it into slices. All joints of roast beef should be cut in even and thin slices. Horseradish, finely scraped, may be served as a garnish; but horseradish sauce is preferable for eating with the beef.

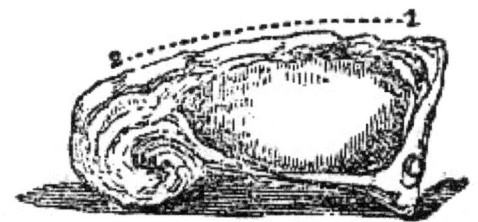

Beef, a Round of.—A round of beef is more easily carved than any other joint of beef, but, to manage it properly, a thin-bladed and very sharp knife is necessary. Off the outside of the joint, at its top, a thick slice should first be cut, so as to leave the surface smooth: then thin and even slices should be cleverly carved in the direction of the line 1 to 2; and with each slice of the lean a delicate morsel of the fat should be served.

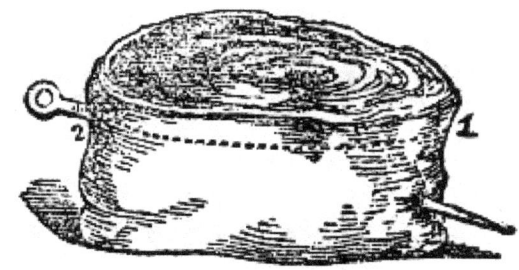

Beef, Sirloin of.—This dish is served differently at various tables, some preferring it to come to table with the fillet, or, as it is usually called, the undercut, uppermost. The reverse way, as shown in the cut, is that most usually adopted. Still the undercut is best eaten when hot; consequently, the carver himself may raise the joint, and cut some slices from the under side, in the direction of from 1 to 2, as the fillet is very much preferred by some eaters. The upper part of the sirloin should be cut in the direction of the line from 5 to 6, and care should be taken to carve it evenly and in thin slices. It will be found a great assistance, in carving this joint well, if the knife be first inserted just above the bone at the bottom, and run sharply along between the bone and meat, and also to divide the meat from the bone in the same way at the side of the joint; the slices will then come away more readily. Some carvers cut the upper side of the sirloin across, as shown by the line from 3 to 4; but this is a wasteful plan, and one not to be recommended. With the sirloin, very finely-scraped horseradish is usually served, and a little given, when liked, to each guest. Horseradish sauce is preferable, however, for serving on the plate, although the scraped horseradish may still be used as a garnish.

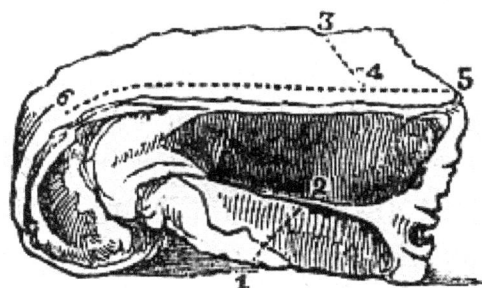

Beef Tongue.—Passing the knife down in the direction of from 1 to 2, a not too thin slice should be helped; and the carving of a tongue may be continued in this way until the best portions of the upper side are served. The fat which lies about the root can be served by turning the tongue, and cutting in the direction of from 3 to 4.

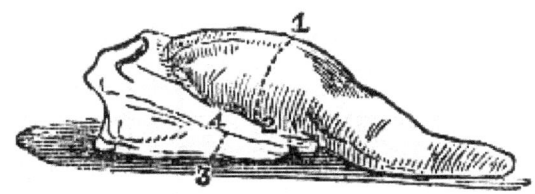

BEEF, Curried.

[Cold Meat Cookery.] *Ingredients.*—A few slices of tolerably lean cold roast or boiled beef, 3 oz. of butter, 2 onions, 1 wineglassful of beer, a dessertspoonful of curry powder. *Mode.*—Cut up the beef into pieces about 1 inch square, put the butter into a stewpan with the onions sliced, and fry them of a light-brown colour. Add all the other ingredients, and stir gently over a brisk fire for about 10 minutes. Should this be thought too dry, more beer, or a spoonful or two of gravy or water, may be added; but a good curry should not be very thin. Place it in a deep dish, with an edging of dry boiled rice, in the same manner as for other curries. *Time.*—10 minutes. *Average cost*, exclusive of the meat, 4*d*. *Seasonable* in winter.

BEEF, Roast Fillet of (Larded).

Ingredients.—About 4 lbs. of the inside fillet of the sirloin, 1 onion, a small bunch of parsley, salt and pepper to taste, sufficient vinegar to cover the meat, glaze, Spanish sauce (*see* Sauce). *Mode.*—Lard the beef with bacon, and put it into a pan with sufficient vinegar to cover it, with an onion sliced, parsley, and seasoning, and let it remain in this pickle for 12 hours. Roast it before a nice clear fire for about 1¼ hour, and, when done, glaze it. Pour some Spanish sauce round the beef, and the remainder serve in a tureen. It may be garnished with Spanish onions boiled and glazed. *Time.*—1¼ hour. *Average cost*, exclusive of the sauce, 4*s*. *Sufficient* for 6 or 8 persons. *Seasonable* at any time.

BEEF, Fricandeau of.

Ingredients.—About 3 lbs. of the inside fillet of the sirloin (a piece of the rump may be substituted for this), pepper and salt to taste, 3 cloves, 2 blades of mace, 6 whole allspice, 1 pint of stock (*see* Stock), or water, 1 glass of sherry, 1 bunch of savoury herbs, 2 shalots, bacon. *Mode.*—Cut some bacon into thin strips, and sprinkle over them a seasoning of pepper and salt, mixed with cloves, mace, and allspice, well pounded. Lard the beef with these, put it into a stewpan with the stock or water, sherry, herbs, shalots, 2 cloves, and more pepper and salt. Stew the meat gently until tender, when take it out, cover it closely, skim off all the fat from the gravy, and strain it. Set it on the fire, and boil, till it becomes a glaze. Glaze the larded side of the beef with this, and serve on sorrel sauce, which is made as follows:—Wash and pick some sorrel, and put it into a stewpan with only the water that hangs about it. Keep stirring, to prevent its burning, and when done, lay it in a sieve to drain. Chop it, and stew it with a small piece of butter and 4 or 5 tablespoonfuls of good gravy, for an hour, and rub it through a sieve. If too acid, add sugar; a little cabbage-lettuce boiled with the sorrel will be found an improvement. *Time.*—2 hours to gently stew the meat. *Average cost*, for this quantity, 4s. *Sufficient* for 6 persons. *Seasonable* at any time.

BEEF, Fried Salt.

[COLD MEAT COOKERY.] *Ingredients.*—A few slices of cold salt beef, pepper to taste, ½ lb. of butter, mashed potatoes. *Mode.*—Cut any part of cold salt beef into thin slices, fry them gently in butter, and season with a little pepper. Have ready some very hot mashed potatoes, lay the slices of beef on them, and garnish with 3 or 4 pickled gherkins. Cold salt beef, warmed in a little liquor from mixed pickle, drained, and served as above, will be found good. *Time.*—About 5 minutes. *Average cost*, exclusive of the meat, 4*d. Seasonable* at any time.

BEEF FRITTERS.

[COLD MEAT COOKERY.] *Ingredients.*—The remains of cold roast beef, pepper and salt to taste, ¾ lb. of flour, ½ pint of water, 2 oz. of butter, the whites of 2 eggs. *Mode.*—Mix very smoothly, and, by degrees, the flour with the above proportion of water; stir in 2 oz. of butter, which must be melted but not oiled, and, just before it is to be used, add the whites of two well-whisked eggs. Should the batter be too thick, more water must be added. Pare down the cold beef into thin shreds, season with pepper and salt, and mix it with the batter. Drop a small quantity at a time into a pan of boiling lard, and fry from 7 to 10 minutes, according to the size. When done on one side, turn and brown them on the other. Let them dry for a minute or two before the fire, and serve on a folded napkin. A small quantity of finely-minced onions, mixed with the batter, is an improvement. *Time.*—From 7 to 10 minutes. *Average cost*, exclusive of the meat, 6*d. Seasonable* at any time.

BEEF, Hashed.

[COLD MEAT COOKERY. 1.] *Ingredients.*—Gravy saved from the meat, 1 teaspoonful of tomato sauce, one teaspoonful of Harvey's sauce, one teaspoonful of good mushroom ketchup, ½ glass of port wine or strong ale, pepper and salt to taste, a little flour to thicken, 1 onion finely minced, a few slices of cold roast beef. *Mode.*—Put all the ingredients but the beef into a stewpan with whatever gravy may have been saved from the meat the day it was roasted; simmer these gently for 10 minutes, then take the stewpan off the fire; let the gravy cool and skim off the fat. Cut the beef into thin slices, dredge them with flour, and lay them in the gravy; let the whole simmer gently for 5 minutes, but not boil, or the meat will be tough and hard. Serve very hot, and garnish with sippets of toasted bread. *Time.*—20 minutes. Average cost, exclusive of the cold meat, 4*d*. *Seasonable* at any time.

[COLD MEAT COOKERY. 2.] *Ingredients.*—The remains of ribs or sirloin of beef, 2 onions, 1 carrot, 1 bunch of savoury herbs, pepper and salt to taste, ½ blade of pounded mace, thickening of flour, rather more than 1 pint of water. *Mode.*—Take off all the meat from the bones of ribs or sirloin of beef; remove the outside brown and gristle; place the meat on one side, and well stew the bones and pieces, with the above ingredients, for about 2 hours, till it becomes a strong gravy, and is reduced to rather more than ½ pint; strain this, thicken with a teaspoonful of flour, and let the gravy cool; skim off all the fat; lay in the meat, let it get hot through, but do not allow it to boil; and garnish with sippets of toasted bread. The gravy should be flavoured as in the preceding recipe. *Time.*—Rather more than 2 hours. *Average cost*, exclusive of the cold meat, 6*d*. *Seasonable* at any time.

Note.—Either of the above recipes may be served in walls of mashed potatoes browned; in which case the sippets should be omitted. *Be careful that hashed meat does not boil, or it will become tough.*

BEEF, Hunter's.

Ingredients.—For a round of beef weighing 25 lbs. allow 3 oz. of saltpetre, 3 oz. of coarse sugar, 1 oz. of cloves, 1 grated nutmeg, ½ oz. of allspice, 1 lb. of salt, ½ lb. bay-salt. *Mode.*—Hang the beef for 2 or 3 days, and remove the bone. Pound spices, salt, &c. in the above proportion, and let them be reduced to the finest powder. Put the beef into a pan, rub all the ingredients well into it, and turn and rub it every day for rather more than a fortnight. When it has been sufficiently long in pickle, wash the meat, bind it up securely with tape, and put it into a pan with ½ pint of water at the bottom; mince some suet, cover the top of the meat with it, and over the pan put a common crust of flour and water; bake for 6 hours, and when cold remove the paste. Save the gravy that flows from it, as it adds greatly to the flavour of hashes, stews, &c. The beef may be glazed and garnished with meat jelly. *Time.*—6 hours. *Seasonable* all the year.

Note.—In salting or pickling beef or pork for family consumption, it not being generally required to be kept for a great length of time, a less quantity of salt and a larger quantity of other matters more adapted to retain mellowness in meat, may be employed, which could not be adopted by the curer of the immense quantities of meat required to be preserved for victualling the shipping of this maritime country. Sugar, which is well known to possess the preserving principle in a very great degree, without the pungency and astringency of salt, may be, and is, very generally used in the preserving of meat for family consumption. Although it acts without corrugating or contracting the fibres of meat, as is the case in the action of salt, and, therefore, does not impair its mellowness, yet its use in sufficient quantities for preservative effect, without the addition of other antiseptics, would impart a flavour not agreeable to the taste of many persons. It may be used, however, together with salt, with the greatest advantage in imparting mildness and mellowness to cured meat, in a proportion of about one part by weight to four of the mixture; and, perhaps, now that sugar is so much lower in price than it was in former years, one of the obstructions to its more frequent use is removed.

BEEF KIDNEY, to Dress.

Ingredients.—1 kidney, clarified butter, pepper and salt to taste, a small quantity of highly-seasoned gravy, 1 tablespoonful of lemon-juice, ¼ teaspoonful of powdered sugar. *Mode.*—Cut the kidneys into neat slices, put them into warm water to soak for two hours, and change the water 2 or 3 times; then lay them on a clean cloth to dry the water from them, place them in a frying-pan with some clarified butter, and fry them of a nice brown; season each side with pepper and salt, put them round the dish, with the gravy in the middle. Before pouring the gravy in the dish, add the lemon-juice and sugar. *Time.*—From 5 to 10 minutes. *Average cost*, 9*d.* each. *Seasonable* at any time.

BEEF KIDNEY, to Dress.

Ingredients.—1 kidney, 1 dessertspoonful of minced parsley, 1 teaspoonful of minced shalot, salt and pepper to taste; ¼ pint of gravy (follow one of the gravy recipes), 3 tablespoonfuls of sherry. *Mode.*—Take off a little of the kidney fat, mince it very fine, and put it in a frying-pan; slice the kidney, sprinkle over it parsley and shalots in the above proportion, add a seasoning of pepper and salt, and fry it of a nice brown. When it is done enough, dredge over a little flour, and pour in the gravy and sherry. Let it just simmer, but not boil any more, or the kidney would harden; serve very hot, and garnish with croûtons. Where the flavour of the shalot is disliked it may be omitted, and a small quantity of savoury herbs substituted for it. *Time.*—From 5 to 10 minutes, according to the thickness of the slices. *Average cost*, 9*d.* each. *Sufficient* for 3 persons. *Seasonable* at any time.

BEEF KIDNEY, to Dress (a more simple method).

Cut the kidneys into thin slices, flour them, and fry of a nice brown. When done, make a gravy in the pan by pouring away the fat, putting in a small piece of butter, ¼ pint of boiling water, pepper and salt, a dessertspoonful of lemon-juice, and a tablespoonful of mushroom ketchup. Let the gravy just boil up, pour over the kidney, and serve.

BEEF MARROW-BONES, Boiled.

MARROW-BONES.

Ingredients.—Bones, a small piece of common paste, a floured cloth. *Mode.*—Have the bones neatly sawed into convenient sizes, and cover the ends with a small piece of common crust, made with flour and water. Over this tie a floured cloth, and place them upright in a saucepan of boiling water, taking care there is sufficient to cover the bones. Boil the bones for 2 hours, remove the cloth and paste, and serve them upright on a napkin with dry toast. Many persons clear the marrow from the bones after they are cooked, spread it over a slice of toast, and add a seasoning of pepper; when served in this manner, it must be very expeditiously sent to table, as it so soon gets cold. *Time.*—2 hours. *Seasonable* at any time.

Note.—Marrow-bones may be baked after preparing them as in the preceding recipe; they should be laid in a deep dish, and baked for 2 hours.

BEEF, Minced.

[COLD MEAT COOKERY.] *Ingredients.*—1 oz. of butter, 1 small onion, 12 tablespoonfuls of gravy left from the meat, 1 tablespoonful of strong ale, 1 teaspoonful of flour, salt and pepper to taste, a few slices of lean roast beef. *Mode.*—Put into a stewpan the butter with an onion chopped fine; add the gravy, ale, and a teaspoonful of flour to thicken; season with pepper and salt, and stir these ingredients over the fire until the onion is a rich brown. Cut (but do not chop) the meat *very fine*, add it to the gravy, stir till quite hot, and serve. Garnish with sippets of toasted bread. Be careful in not allowing the gravy to boil after the meat is added, as it would render it hard and tough. *Time.*—About ½ hour. *Average cost*, exclusive of the meat, 3*d*. *Seasonable* at any time.

BEEF, Minced Collops of (an Entrée).

Ingredients.—1 lb. of rump-steak, salt and pepper to taste, 2 oz. of butter, 1 onion minced, ¼ pint of water, 1 tablespoonful of Harvey's sauce, or lemon-juice, or mushroom ketchup; 1 small bunch of savoury herbs. *Mode.*—Mince the beef and onion very small, and fry the latter in butter until of a pale brown. Put all the ingredients together in a stewpan, and boil gently for about 10 minutes; garnish with sippets of toasted bread, and serve very hot. *Time.*—10 minutes. *Average cost*, 1s. per lb. *Sufficient* for 2 or 3 persons. *Seasonable* at any time.

BEEF, Miroton of.

[Cold Meat Cookery.] *Ingredients.*—A few slices of cold roast beef, 3 oz. of butter, salt and pepper to taste, 3 onions, ½ pint of gravy. *Mode.*—Slice the onions and put them into the frying-pan with the cold beef and butter; place it over the fire, and keep turning and stirring the ingredients to prevent them burning. When a pale brown, add the gravy and seasoning; let it simmer for a few minutes, and serve very hot. The dish is excellent and economical. *Time.*—5 minutes. *Average cost*, exclusive of the meat, 6d. *Seasonable* at any time.

BEEF OLIVES.

Ingredients.—2 lbs. of rump-steak, 1 egg, 1 tablespoonful of minced savoury herbs, pepper and salt to taste, 1 pint of stock, 2 or 3 slices of bacon, 2 tablespoonfuls of any kind of store sauce, a slight thickening of butter and flour. Mode.—Have the steaks cut rather thin, beat them to make them level, cut them into 6 or 7 pieces, brush over with egg, and sprinkle with herbs, which should be very finely minced; season with pepper and salt, roll up the pieces tightly, and fasten with a small skewer. Put the stock in a stewpan that will exactly hold the ingredients, for, by being pressed together, they will keep their shape better; lay in the rolls of meat, cover them with the bacon, cut in thin slices, and over that put a piece of paper. Stew them very *gently* for full 2 hours; for the slower they are done the better. Take them out, remove the skewers, thicken the gravy with butter and flour, and flavour with any store sauce that may be preferred. Give one boil, pour over the meat, and serve. *Time.*—2 hours. *Average cost*, 1s. per pound. *Sufficient* for 4 or 5 persons. *Seasonable* at any time.

BEEF OLIVES (Economical).

[COLD MEAT COOKERY.] *Ingredients.*—The remains of underdone cold roast beef, bread-crumbs, 1 shalot finely minced, pepper and salt to taste, gravy made from the beef bones, thickening of butter and flour, 1 tablespoonful of mushroom ketchup. *Mode.*—Cut some slices of underdone roast beef about half an inch thick; sprinkle over them some bread-crumbs, minced shalot, and a little of the fat and seasoning; roll them, and fasten with a small skewer. Have ready some gravy made from the beef bones; put in the pieces of meat, and stew them till tender, which will be in about 1¼ hour, or rather longer. Arrange the meat in a dish, thicken and flavour the gravy, and pour it over the meat, when it is ready to serve. *Time.*—1½ hour. *Average cost*, exclusive of the beef, 2d. *Seasonable* at any time.

BEEF PALATES, to Dress (an Entrée).

Ingredients.—4 palates, sufficient gravy to cover them, cayenne to taste, 1 tablespoonful of mushroom ketchup, 1 tablespoonful of pickled-onion liquor, thickening of butter and flour. *Mode.*—Wash the palates, and put them into a stewpan, with sufficient water to cover them, and let them boil until perfectly tender, or until the upper skin may be easily peeled off. Have ready sufficient gravy to cover them; add a good seasoning of cayenne, and thicken with a little butter kneaded with flour; let it boil up, and skim. Cut the palates into square pieces, put them in the gravy, and let them simmer gently for ½ hour; add ketchup and onion-liquor, give one boil, and serve. *Time.*—From 3 to 5 hours to boil the palates. *Sufficient* for 4 persons. *Seasonable* at any time.

Note.—Palates may be dressed in various ways with good onion sauce, tomato sauce, &c., &c., and may also be served in a *vol-au-vent*; but the above will be found a more simple method of dressing them.

BEEF PICKLE. (This may also be used for any kind of Meat, Tongues, or Hams.)

Ingredients.—6 lbs. of salt, 2 lbs. of fine sugar, 3 oz. of powdered saltpetre, 3 gallons of spring water. *Mode.*—Boil all the ingredients gently together, so long as any scum or impurity arises, which carefully remove;

when quite cold, pour it over the meat, every part of which must be covered with the brine. This may be used for pickling any kind of meat, and may be kept for some time, if boiled up occasionally with an addition of the ingredients. *Time.*—A ham should be kept in pickle for a fortnight; a piece of beef weighing 14 lbs., 12 or 15 days; a tongue, 10 days or a fortnight.

Note.—For salting and pickling meat, it is a good plan to rub in only half the quantity of salt directed, and to let it remain for a day or two to disgorge and effectually to get rid of the blood and slime; then rub in the remainder of the salt and other ingredients, and proceed as above. This rule may be applied to all recipes for salting and pickling meat.

BEEF, Potted.

JAR FOR POTTED MEATS.

[COLD MEAT COOKERY. 1.] *Ingredients.*—2 lbs. of lean beef, 1 tablespoonful of water, ¼ lb. of butter, a seasoning to taste of salt, cayenne, pounded mace, and black pepper. *Mode.*—Procure a nice piece of lean beef, as free as possible from gristle, skin, &c., and put it into a jar (if at hand, one with a lid) with 1 tablespoonful of water. Cover it *closely*, and put the jar into a saucepan of boiling water, letting the water come within 2 inches of the top of the jar. Boil gently for 3½ hours, then take the beef, chop it very small with a chopping-knife, and pound it thoroughly in a mortar. Mix with it by degrees all, or a portion, of the gravy that will have run from it, and a little clarified butter; add the seasoning, put it in small pots for use, and cover with a little butter just warmed and poured over. If much gravy is added to it, it will keep but a short time; on the contrary, if a large proportion of butter is used, it may be preserved for some time. *Time.*—3½ hours. *Average cost,* for this quantity, 1*s.* 10*d.* *Seasonable* at any time.

[COLD MEAT COOKERY. 2.] *Ingredients.*—The remains of cold roast or boiled beef, ¼ lb. of butter, cayenne to taste, 2 blades of pounded mace.

Mode.—The outside slices of boiled beef may, with a little trouble, be converted into a very nice addition to the breakfast-table. Cut up the meat into small pieces and pound it well, with a little butter, in a mortar; add a seasoning of cayenne and mace, and be very particular that the latter spice is reduced to the finest powder. When all the ingredients are thoroughly mixed, put them into glass or earthen potting-pots, and pour on the top a coating of clarified butter. *Seasonable* at any time.

Note.—If cold *roast* beef is used, remove all pieces of gristle and dry outside pieces, as these do not pound well.

BEEF RAGOÛT.

[COLD MEAT COOKERY.] *Ingredients.*—About 2 lbs. of cold roast beef, 6 onions, pepper, salt, and mixed spices to taste; ½ pint of boiling water, 3 tablespoonfuls of gravy. *Mode.*—Cut the beef into rather large pieces, and put them into a stewpan with the onions, which must be sliced. Season well with pepper, salt, and mixed spices, and pour over about ½ pint of boiling water, and gravy in the above proportion (gravy saved from the meat answers the purpose); let the whole stew very gently for about 2 hours, and serve with pickled walnuts, gherkins, or capers, just warmed in the gravy. *Time.*—2 hours. *Average cost,* exclusive of the meat, 4*d*. *Seasonable* at any time.

BEEF, Rib-bones of (a pretty Dish).

[COLD MEAT COOKERY.] *Ingredients.*—Ribs of beef bones, 1 onion chopped fine, a few slices of carrot and turnip, ¼ pint of gravy. *Mode.*—The bones for this dish should have left on them a slight covering of meat; saw them into pieces 3 inches long; season them with pepper and salt, and put them into a stewpan with the remaining ingredients. Stew gently, until the vegetables are tender, and serve on a flat dish within walls of mashed potatoes, *Time.*—¾ hour. *Average cost,* exclusive of the bones, 2*d*. *Seasonable* at any time.

BEEF, Roast Ribs of.

Ingredients.—Beef, a little salt. *Mode.*—The fore-rib is considered the primest roasting piece, but the middle-rib is considered the most economical. Let the meat be well hung (should the weather permit), having previously cut off the ends of the bones, which should be salted for a few days, and then boiled. Put the meat down to a nice clear fire, with some clean dripping in the pan, dredge the joint with a little flour, and keep continually basting it all the time it is cooking. Sprinkle some fine salt over it (this must never be done until the joint is dished, as it draws the juices from the meat); pour the dripping from the pan, put in a little boiling water, and *strain* the gravy over the meat. Garnish with tufts of scraped horseradish, and send horseradish sauce to table with it. A Yorkshire pudding (*see* [Puddings](#)) sometimes accompanies this dish, and, if lightly made and well cooked, will be found a very agreeable addition. *Time.*—10 lbs. of beef, 2½ hours; 14 to 16 lbs., from 3½ to 4 hours. *Average cost,* 9*d.* per lb. *Sufficient.*—A joint of 10 lbs. sufficient for 8 or 9 persons. *Seasonable* at any time.

BEEF, Roast Ribs of, Boned and Rolled (a very convenient Joint for a small Family).

Ingredients.—1 or 2 ribs of beef. *Mode.*—Choose a fine rib of beef, and have it cut according to the weight you require, either wide or narrow. Bone and roll the meat round, secure it with wooden skewers, and, if necessary, bind it round with a piece of tape. Spit the beef firmly, or, if a bottle-jack is used, put the joint on the hook, and place it *near* a nice clear fire. Let it remain so till the outside of the meat is set, when draw it to a distance, and keep continually basting until the meat is done, which can be ascertained by the steam from it drawing towards the fire. As this joint is solid, rather more than ¼ hour must be allowed for each lb. Remove the skewers, put in a plated or silver one, and send the joint to table with gravy in the dish, and garnish with tufts of horseradish. Horseradish sauce is a great improvement to roast beef. *Time.*—For 10 lbs. of the rolled ribs, 3 hours (as the joint is very solid, we have allowed an extra ½ hour); for 6 lbs., 1½ hour. *Average cost,* 9*d.* per lb. *Sufficient.*—A joint of 10 lbs. for 6 or 8 persons. *Seasonable* all the year.

Note.—When the weight exceeds 10 lbs., we would not advise the above method of boning or rolling; only in the case of 1 or 2 ribs, when the joint cannot stand upright in the dish, and would look awkwardly. The bones should be put on with a few vegetables and herbs, and made into stock.

BEEF RISSOLES.

[COLD MEAT COOKERY.] *Ingredients.*—The remains of cold roast beef; to each pound of meat allow ¾ lb. of bread-crumbs, salt and pepper to taste, a few chopped savoury herbs, ½ a teaspoonful of minced lemon-peel, 1 or 2 eggs, according to the quantity of meat. *Mode.*—Mince the beef very fine, which should be rather lean, and mix with this bread-crumbs, herbs, seasoning, and lemon-peel, in the above proportion, to each pound of meat. Make all into a thick paste with 1 or 2 eggs; divide into balls or cones, and fry a rich brown. Garnish the dish with fried parsley, and send to table some good brown gravy in a tureen. Instead of garnishing with fried parsley, gravy may be poured in the dish round the rissoles; in this case, it will not be necessary to send any in a tureen. *Time.*—From 5 to 10 minutes, according to size. *Average cost*, exclusive of the meat, 5*d*. *Seasonable* at any time.

BEEF, Rolled, to eat like Hare.

Ingredients.—About 5 lbs. of the inside of the sirloin, 2 glasses of port wine, 2 glasses of vinegar, a small quantity of forcemeat, 1 teaspoonful of pounded allspice. *Mode.*—Take the inside of a large sirloin, soak it in 1 glass of port wine and 1 glass of vinegar, mixed, and let it remain for 2 days. Make a forcemeat (*see* FORCEMEAT), lay it on the meat, and bind it up securely. Roast it before a nice clear fire, and baste it with 1 glass each of port wine and vinegar, with which mix a teaspoonful of pounded allspice. Serve, with a good gravy in the dish, and send red-currant jelly to table with it. *Time.*—A piece of 5 lbs., about 1½ hour before a brisk fire. *Average cost*, for this quantity, 5*s*. 4*d*. *Sufficient* for 4 persons. *Seasonable* at any time.

BEEF ROLLS.

[COLD MEAT COOKERY.] *Ingredients.*—The remains of cold roast or boiled beef, seasoning to taste of salt, pepper, and minced herbs; puff paste.

Mode.—Mince the beef tolerably fine with a *small* amount of its own fat; add a seasoning of pepper, salt, and chopped herbs; put the whole into a roll of puff paste, and bake for ½ hour, or rather longer, should the roll be very large. Beef patties may be made of cold meat, by mincing and seasoning beef as directed above, and baking in a rich puff paste in patty-tins. *Time.*— ½ hour. *Seasonable* at any time.

BEEF, Boiled Round of.

Ingredients.—Beef, water. *Mode.*—As a whole round of beef, generally speaking, is too large for small families, and very seldom required, we here give the recipe for dressing a portion of the silver side of the round. Take from 12 to 16 lbs., after it has been in salt about 10 days; just wash off the salt, skewer it up in a nice round-looking form, and bind it with tape to keep the skewers in their places. Put it in a saucepan of boiling water, set it upon a good fire, and when it begins to boil, carefully remove all scum from the surface, as, if this is not attended to, it sinks on to the meat, and, when brought to table, presents a very unsightly appearance. After it is well skimmed, draw the pot to the corner of the fire, allow the liquor to cool, then let the beef simmer very gently until done. Remove the tape and skewers, which should be replaced by a silver one; pour over a little of the pot-liquor, and garnish with carrots. Carrots, turnips, parsnips, and sometimes suet dumplings, accompany this dish; and these may all be boiled with the beef. The pot-liquor should be saved, and converted into pea-soup; and the outside slices, which are generally hard, and of an uninviting appearance, may be cut off before being sent to table, and potted. These make an excellent relish for the breakfast or luncheon table. *Time.*— Part of a round of beef weighing 12 lbs., about 3 hours after the water boils. *Average cost*, 8d. per lb. *Sufficient* for 10 persons. *Seasonable* all the year, but more suitable for winter.

Soyer's Recipe for Preserving the Gravy in Salt Meat, when it is to be served Cold.—Fill two tubs with cold water, into which throw a few pounds of rough ice; and when the meat is done, put it into one of the tubs of ice-water; let it remain 1 minute, when take out, and put it into the other tub. Fill the first tub again with water, and continue this process for about

20 minutes; then set it upon a dish, and let it remain until quite cold. When cut, the fat will be as white as possible, besides having saved the whole of the gravy. If there is no ice, spring water will answer the same purpose, but will require to be more frequently changed.

Note.—The brisket and rump may be boiled by the above recipe; of course allowing more or less time, according to the size of the joint.

BEEF, Miniature Round of (an excellent Dish for a small Family).

Ingredients.—From 5 to 10 lbs. of ribs of beef, sufficient brine to cover the meat. *Mode.*—Choose a fine rib, have the bone removed, rub some salt over the inside, and skewer the meat up into a nice round form, and bind it with tape. Put it into sufficient brine to cover it (*see* BEEF PICKLE), and let it remain for 6 days, turning the meat every day. When required to be dressed, drain from the pickle, and put the meat into very hot water; boil it rapidly for a few minutes, then draw the pot to the side of the fire, and simmer the beef very gently until done. Remove the skewer, and replace it by a plated or silver one. Carrots and turnips should be served with this dish, and may be boiled with the meat. *Time.*—A small round of 8 lbs., about 2 hours after the water boils; one of 12 lbs., about 3 hours. *Average cost*, 9*d.* per lb. *Sufficient* for 6 persons. *Seasonable* at any time.

Note.—Should the joint be very small, 4 or 5 days will be sufficient time to salt it.

BEEF, to Pickle part of a Round, for Hanging.

Ingredients.—For 14 lbs. of a round of beef allow 1½ lb. of salt, ½ oz. of powdered saltpetre; or, 1 lb. of salt, ½ lb. of sugar, ½ oz. of powdered saltpetre. *Mode.*—Rub in, and sprinkle either of the above mixtures on 14 lbs. of meat. Keep it in an earthenware pan, or a deep wooden tray, and turn twice a week during 3 weeks; then bind up the beef tightly with coarse linen tape, and hang it in a kitchen in which a fire is constantly kept, for 3 weeks. Pork, hams, and bacon may be cured in a similar way, but will require double the quantity of the salting mixture; and, if not smoke-dried, they should be taken down from hanging after 3 or 4 weeks, and afterwards kept in boxes or tubs, amongst dry oat-husks. *Time.*—2 or 3 weeks to remain in the brine, to be hung 3 weeks. *Seasonable* at any time.

Note.—The meat may be boiled fresh from this pickle, instead of smoking it.

BEEF SAUSAGES.

Ingredients.—To every lb. of suet allow 2 lbs. of lean beef; seasoning to taste of salt, pepper, and mixed spices. *Mode.*—Clear the suet from skin, and chop that and the beef as finely as possible; season with pepper, salt, and spices, and mix the whole well together. Make it into flat cakes, and fry of a nice brown. Many persons pound the meat in a mortar after it is chopped, but this is not necessary when the meat is minced finely. *Time.*—10 minutes. *Average cost,* for this quantity, 1*s.* 6*d. Seasonable* at any time.

BEEF, Roast Sirloin of.

ROAST SIRLOIN OF BEEF.

Ingredients.—Beef, a little salt. *Mode.*—As a joint cannot be well roasted without a good fire, see that it is well made up about ¾ hour before it is required, so that when the joint is put down, it is clear and bright. Choose a nice sirloin, the weight of which should not exceed 16 lbs., as the outside would be too much done, whilst the inside would not be done enough. Spit it or hook it on to the jack firmly, dredge it slightly with flour, and place it near the fire at first. Then draw it to a distance, and keep continually basting until the meat is done. Dish the meat, sprinkle a small quantity of salt over it, empty the dripping-pan of all the dripping, pour in some boiling water, stir it about, and *strain* over the meat. Garnish with tufts of horseradish, and send horseradish sauce and Yorkshire pudding to table with it. *Time.*—A sirloin of 10 lbs., 2½ hours; 14 to 16 lbs., about 4 or

4½ hours. *Average cost*, 8½d. per lb. *Sufficient*.—A joint of 10 lbs. for 8 or 9 persons. *Seasonable* at any time. The rump, round, and other pieces of beef are roasted in the same manner, allowing for solid joints ¼ hour to every lb.

Note.—The above is the usual method of roasting meat; but to have it in perfection and the juices kept in, the meat should at first be laid *close* to the fire, and when the outside is set and firm, drawn away to a good distance, and then left to roast very slowly. Where economy is studied, this plan would not answer, as the meat requires to be at the fire double the time of the ordinary way of cooking; consequently, double the quantity of fuel would be consumed.

BEEF, Sliced and Broiled (a pretty Dish).

[COLD MEAT COOKERY.] *Ingredients.*—A few slices of cold roast beef, 4 or 5 potatoes, a thin batter, pepper and salt to taste. *Mode.*—Pare the potatoes as you would peel an apple; fry the parings in a thin batter seasoned with salt and pepper, until they are of a light brown colour, and place them on a dish over some slices of beef, which should be nicely seasoned and broiled. *Time.*—5 minutes to broil the meat. *Seasonable* at any time.

BEEF, Spiced (to serve Cold).

Ingredients.—14 lbs. of the thick flank or rump of beef, ½ lb. of coarse sugar, 1 oz. of saltpetre, ¼ lb. of pounded allspice, 1 lb. of common salt. *Mode.*—Rub the sugar well into the beef, and let it lie for 12 hours; then rub the saltpetre and allspice, both of which should be pounded, over the meat, and let it remain for another 12 hours; then rub in the salt. Turn daily in the liquor for a fortnight, soak it for a few hours in water, dry with a cloth, cover with a coarse paste, put a little water at the bottom of the pan, and bake in a moderate oven for 4 hours. If it is not covered with a paste, be careful to put the beef into a deep vessel, and cover with a plate, or it will be too crisp. During the time the meat is in the oven it should be turned once or twice. *Time.*—4 hours. *Average cost*, 7d. per lb. *Seasonable* at any time.

BEEF, Stewed. (A Polish Dish.)

Ingredients.—A thick beef or rump-steak of about 2 lbs., an onion, some bread-crumbs, pepper and salt, ¼ lb. of butter. *Mode.*—Mince the onion fine, mix it with the bread, pepper, and salt; make deep incisions in the beef, but do not cut it through; fill the spaces with the bread, &c. Roll up the steak and put it in a stewpan with the butter; let it stew very gently for more than two hours; serve it with its own gravy, thickened with a little flour, and flavoured, as may be required, either with tomato sauce, ketchup, or Harvey's sauce. *Time.*—About 2 hours, or rather more. *Average cost*, 2s. 6d. *Sufficient* for 4 persons. *Seasonable* at any time.

BEEF, Stewed Rump of.

Ingredients.—½ rump of beef, sufficient stock to cover it, 4 tablespoonfuls of vinegar, 2 tablespoonfuls of ketchup, 1 bunch of savoury herbs, 2 onions, 12 cloves, pepper and salt to taste, thickening of butter and flour, 1 glass of port wine. *Mode.*—Cut out the bone, sprinkle the meat with a little cayenne (this must be sparingly used), and bind and tie it firmly up with tape; put it into a stewpan with sufficient stock to cover it, add vinegar, ketchup, herbs, onions, cloves, and seasonings in the above proportions, and simmer very gently for 4 or 5 hours, or until the meat is perfectly tender, which may be ascertained by piercing it with a thin skewer. When done, remove the tape, lay it into a deep dish, which keep hot; strain and skim the gravy, thicken it with butter and flour, add a glass of port wine and any flavouring to make the gravy rich and palatable; let it boil up, pour over the meat, and serve. This dish may be very much enriched by garnishing with forcemeat balls, or filling up the space whence the bone is taken with a good forcemeat; sliced carrots, turnips, and onions boiled with the meat are also a great improvement, and, where expense is not objected to, it may be glazed. This, however, is not necessary where a good gravy is poured round and over the meat. *Time.*—½ rump stewed gently from 4 to 5 hours. *Average cost*, 10d. per lb. *Sufficient* for 8 or 10 persons. *Seasonable* at any time.

Note.—A stock or gravy in which to boil the meat may be made of the bone and trimmings, by boiling them with water, and adding carrots, onions, turnips, and a bunch of sweet herbs. To make this dish richer and more savoury, half-roast the rump, and afterwards stew it in strong stock and a little Madeira. This is an expensive method, and is not, after all, much better than a plainer-dressed joint.

BEEF, Stewed Shin of.

Ingredients.—A shin of beef, 1 head of celery, 1 onion, a faggot of savoury herbs, ½ teaspoonful of allspice, ½ teaspoonful of whole black pepper, 4 carrots, 12 button onions, 2 turnips, thickening of butter and flour, 3 tablespoonfuls of mushroom ketchup, 2 tablespoonfuls of port wine; pepper and salt to taste. *Mode.*—Have the bone sawn into 4 or 5 pieces, cover with hot water, bring it to a boil, and remove any scum that may rise to the surface. Put in the celery, onion, herbs, spice, and seasoning, and simmer very gently until the meat is tender. Peel the vegetables, cut them into any shape fancy may dictate, and boil them with the onions until tender; lift out the beef, put it on a dish, which keep hot, and thicken with butter and flour as much of the liquor as will be wanted for gravy; keep stirring till it boils, then strain and skim. Put the gravy back in the stewpan, add the seasoning, port wine, and ketchup, give one boil, and pour it over the beef; garnish with the boiled carrots, turnips and onions. *Time.*—The meat to be stewed about 4 hours. *Average cost*, 5*d.* per lb. with bone. *Sufficient* for 7 or 8 persons. *Seasonable* at any time.

BEEF-TEA.

Ingredients.—1 lb. of lean gravy-beef, 1½ pint of water, 1 saltspoonful of salt. *Mode.*—Have the meat cut without fat and bone, and choose a nice fleshy piece. Cut it into small pieces about the size of dice, and put it into a clean saucepan. Add the water *cold* to it; put it on the fire, and bring it to the boiling-point; then skim well. Put in the salt when the water boils, and *simmer* the beef-tea *gently* from ½ to ¾ hour, removing any more scum should it appear on the surface. Strain the tea through a hair sieve, and set it by in a cool place. When wanted for use, remove every particle of fat from the top; warm up as much as may be required, adding, if necessary, a little more salt. This preparation is simple beef-tea, and is to be administered to those invalids to whom flavourings and seasonings are not allowed. When the patient is very weak, use double the quantity of meat to the same proportion of water. Should the invalid be able to take the tea prepared in a more palatable manner, it is easy to make it so by following the directions in Soyer's recipe, which is an admirable one for making savoury beef-tea. Beef-tea is always better when made the day before it is wanted, and then warmed up. It is a good plan to put the tea into a small cup or basin, and to place this basin in a saucepan of boiling water. When the tea is hot, it is ready to serve. *Time.*—½ to ¾ hour. *Average cost*, 6*d.* per pint. *Sufficient.*—Allow 1 lb. of meat for a pint of *good* beef-tea.

BEEF-TEA, Baked.

Ingredients.—1 lb. of fleshy beef, 1 pint of water, ½ saltspoonful of salt. *Mode.*—Cut the beef into small square pieces, after trimming off all the fat, and put it into a baking-jar (these jars are sold expressly for the purpose of making soups, gravies, &c., in the oven, and are arranged with tightly-fitting lids), with the above proportion of water and salt; close the jar well, place it in a warm but not hot oven, and bake for 3 or 4 hours. When the oven is very fierce in the day-time, it is a good plan to put the jar in at night, and let it remain till next morning, when the tea will be done. It should be strained, and put by in a cool place until wanted. It may also be flavoured with an onion, a clove, and a few sweet herbs, &c., when the stomach is sufficiently strong to take these. *Time.*—3 or 4 hours, or to be left in the oven all night. *Average cost*, 6*d.* per pint. *Sufficient.*—Allow 1 lb. of meat for 1 pint of good beef-tea.

BEEF-TEA, Savoury (Soyer's Recipe).

Ingredients.—1 lb. of solid beef, 1 oz. of butter, 1 clove, 2 button onions or ½ a large one, 1 saltspoonful of salt, 1 quart of water. *Mode.*—Cut the beef into very small dice; put it into a stewpan with the butter, clove, onion, and salt; stir the meat round over the fire for a few minutes until it produces a thin gravy, then add the water, and let it simmer gently from ½ to ¾ of an hour, skimming off every particle of fat. When done, strain it through a sieve, and put it by in a cool place until required. The same, if wanted quite plain, is done by merely omitting the vegetables, salt, and clove; the butter cannot be objectionable, as it is taken out in skimming. *Time.*—½ to ¾ hour.

Average cost, 8*d.* per pint. *Sufficient.*—Allow 1 lb. of beef to make 1 pint of good beef-tea.

Note.—The meat left from beef-tea may be boiled a little longer, and pounded with spices, &c., for potting. It makes a very nice breakfast dish.

BEETROOT, Boiled.

Ingredients.—Beetroot; boiling water. *Mode.*—When large, young, and juicy, this vegetable makes a very excellent addition to winter salads, and may easily be converted into an economical and quickly-made pickle. (*See* BEETROOT, PICKLED.) Beetroot is more frequently served cold than hot: when the latter mode is preferred, melted butter should be sent to table with it. It may also be stewed with button onions, or boiled and served with roasted onions. Wash the beets thoroughly; but do not prick or break the skin before they are cooked, as they would lose their beautiful colour in boiling. Put them into boiling water, and let them boil until tender, keeping them well covered. If to be served hot, remove the peel quickly, cut the beetroot into thick slices, and send to table melted butter. For salads, pickle, &c., let the root cool, then peel, and cut it into slices. *Time.*—Small beetroot, 1½ to 2 hours; large, 2½ to 3 hours. *Average cost*, in full season, 2*d.* each. *Seasonable.*—May be had at any time.

BEETROOT, Pickled.

Ingredients.—Sufficient vinegar to cover the beets, 2 oz. of whole pepper, 2 oz. of allspice to each gallon of vinegar. *Mode.*—Wash the beets free from dirt, and be very careful not to prick the outside skin, or they would lose their beautiful colour. Put them into boiling water, let them simmer gently, and when about three parts done, which will be in 1½ hour, take them out and let them cool. Boil the vinegar with pepper and allspice, in the above proportion, for 10 minutes, and when cold, pour it on the beets, which must be peeled and cut into slices about ½ inch thick. Cover with bladder to exclude the air, and in a week they will be fit for use.

BISCUITS, Crisp.

Ingredients.—1 lb. of flour, the yolk of 1 egg, milk. *Mode.*—Mix the flour and the yolk of the egg with sufficient milk to make the whole into a very stiff paste; beat it well, and knead it until it is perfectly smooth. Roll the paste out *very thin*; with a round cutter shape it into small biscuits, and bake them a nice brown in a slow oven from 12 to 18 minutes. *Time.*—12 to 18 minutes. *Average cost*, 4d. *Seasonable* at any time.

BISCUITS, Dessert, which may be flavoured with Ground Ginger, Cinnamon, &c.

Ingredients.—1 lb. of flour, ½ lb. of butter, ½ lb. of sifted sugar, the yolks of 6 eggs, flavouring to taste. *Mode.*—Put the butter into a basin; warm it, but do not allow it to oil; then with the hand beat it to a cream. Add the flour by degrees, then the sugar and flavouring, and moisten the whole with the yolks of the eggs, which should previously be well beaten. When all the ingredients are thoroughly incorporated, drop the mixture from a spoon on to a buttered paper, leaving a distance between each cake, for they spread as soon as they begin to get warm. Bake in rather a slow oven from 12 to 18 minutes, and do not let the biscuits acquire too much colour. In making the above quantity, half may be flavoured with ground ginger and the other half with essence of lemon or currants, to make a variety. With whatever the preparation is flavoured, so are the biscuits called, and an endless variety may be made in this manner. *Time.*—12 to 18 minutes, or rather longer, in a very slow oven. *Average cost*, 1s. 6d. *Sufficient* to make from 3 to 4 dozen cakes. *Seasonable* at any time.

BISCUITS, Simple Hard.

Ingredients.—To every lb. of flour allow 2 oz. of butter, about ½ pint of skimmed milk. *Mode.*—Warm the butter in milk until the former is dissolved, and then mix it with the flour into a very stiff paste; beat it with a rolling-pin until the dough looks perfectly smooth. Roll it out thin; cut it with the top of a glass into round biscuits; prick them well, and bake them from 6 to 10 minutes. The above is the proportion of milk which we think would convert the flour into a stiff paste; but should it be found too much, an extra spoonful or two of flour must be put in. These biscuits are very nice for the cheese course. *Time.*—6 to 10 minutes. *Seasonable* at any time.

ROAST BLACK-COCK.

BLACK-COCK, to Roast.

Ingredients.—Black-cock, butter, toast. *Mode.*—Let these birds hang for a few days, or they will be tough and tasteless, if not well kept. Pluck and draw them, and wipe the insides and outsides with a damp cloth, as washing spoils the flavour. Cut off the heads, and truss them, the same as a roast fowl, cutting off the toes, and scalding and peeling the feet. Trussing them with the head on, as shown in the engraving, is still practised by many cooks, but the former method is now considered the best. Put them down to a brisk fire, well baste them with butter, and serve with a piece of toast under, and a good gravy and bread sauce. After trussing, some cooks cover the breast with vine-leaves and slices of bacon, and then roast them. They should be served in the same manner and with the same accompaniments as with the plainly-roasted birds. *Time.*—45 to 50 minutes. *Average cost*, from 5*s.* to 6*s.* the brace; but seldom bought. *Sufficient,*—2 or 3 for a dish. *Seasonable* from the middle of August to the end of December.

BLACK-COCK, to Carve.

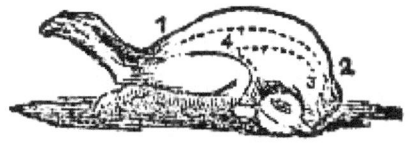

BLACK-COCK.

Skilful carving of game undoubtedly adds to the pleasure of the guests at a dinner-table; for game seems pre-eminently to be composed of such delicate limbs and tender flesh that an inapt practitioner appears to more disadvantage when mauling these pretty and favourite dishes, than larger and more robust *pièces de résistance*. This bird is variously served with or without the head on; and, although we do not personally object to the appearance of the head as shown in the woodcut, yet it seems to be more in vogue to serve it without. The carving is not difficult, but should be elegantly and deftly done. Slices from the breast, cut in the direction of the dotted line from 2 to 1, should be taken off, the merrythought displaced, and the leg and wing removed by running the knife along from 3 to 4, reserving the thigh, which is considered a great delicacy, for the most honoured guests, some of whom may also esteem the brains of this bird.

BLANCMANGE (a Supper Dish).

Ingredients.—1 pint of new milk, 1¼ oz. of isinglass, the rind of ½ lemon, ¼ lb. of loaf sugar, 10 bitter almonds, ½ oz. of sweet almonds, 1 pint of cream. *Mode.*—Put the milk into a saucepan, with the isinglass, lemon-rind, and sugar, and let these ingredients stand by the side of the fire until the milk is well flavoured; add the almonds, which should be blanched and pounded in a mortar to a paste, and let the milk just boil up; strain it through a fine sieve or muslin into a jug, add the cream, and stir the mixture occasionally until nearly cold. Let it stand for a few minutes, then pour it into the mould, which should be previously oiled with the purest salad-oil, or dipped in cold water. There will be a sediment at the bottom of the jug, which must not be poured into the mould, as, when turned out, it would very much disfigure the appearance of the blancmange. This blancmange may be made very much richer by using 1½ pint of cream, and melting the isinglass in ½ pint of boiling water. The flavour may also be very much varied by adding bay-leaves, laurel-leaves, or essence of vanilla, instead of the lemon-rind and almonds. Noyeau, Maraschino, Curaçoa, or any favourite liqueur, added in small proportions, very much enhances the flavour of this always favourite dish. In turning it out, just loosen the edges of the blancmange from the mould, place a dish on it, and turn it quickly over: it should come out easily, and the blancmange have a smooth glossy appearance when the mould is oiled, which it frequently has not when it is only dipped in water. It may be garnished as fancy dictates. *Time.*—About 1½ hour to steep the lemon-rind and almonds in the milk. *Average cost*, with cream at 1*s.* per pint, 3*s.* 6*d. Sufficient* to fill a quart mould. *Seasonable* at any time.

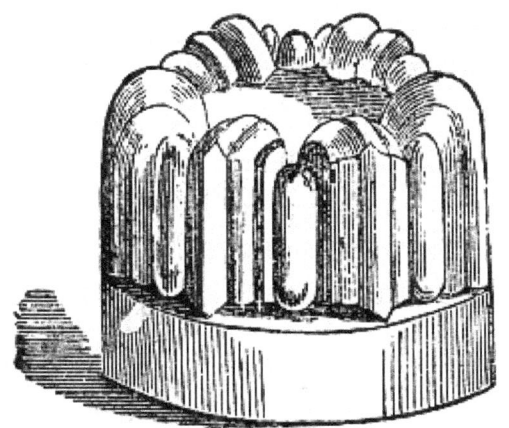

BLANC-MANGE MOULD.

BLANCMANGE, Cheap.

Ingredients.—¼ lb. of sugar, 1 quart of milk, 1½ oz. of isinglass, the rind of ½ lemon, 4 laurel-leaves. *Mode.*—Put all the ingredients into a lined saucepan, and boil gently until the isinglass is dissolved; taste it occasionally to ascertain when it is sufficiently flavoured with the laurel-leaves; then take them out, and keep stirring the mixture over the fire for about 10 minutes. Strain it through a fine sieve into a jug, and, when nearly cold, pour it into a well-oiled mould, omitting the sediment at the bottom. Turn it out carefully on a dish, and garnish with preserves, bright jelly, or a compôte of fruit. *Time.*—Altogether, ½ hour. *Average cost,* 8*d.* *Sufficient* to fill a quart mould. *Seasonable* at any time.

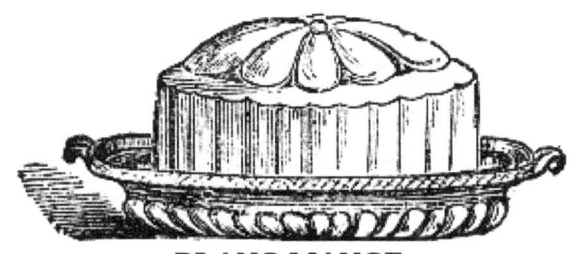

BLANC-MANGE.

BOUDIN à la REINE (an Entrée; M. Ude's Recipe).

Ingredients.—The remains of cold roast fowls, 1 pint of Béchamel, salt and cayenne to taste, egg and bread-crumbs. *Mode.*—Take the breasts and nice white meat from the fowls; cut it into small dice of an equal size, and throw them into some good Béchamel (*see* Béchamel); season with salt and cayenne, and put the mixture into a dish to cool. When this preparation is quite cold, cut it into 2 equal parts, which should be made into boudins of a long shape, the size of the dish they are intended to be served on; roll them in flour, egg and bread-crumb them, and be careful that the ends are well covered with the crumbs, otherwise they will break in the frying-pan; fry them a nice colour, put them before the fire to drain the greasy moisture from them, and serve with the remainder of the Béchamel poured round: this should be thinned with a little stock. *Time.*—10 minutes to fry the boudins. *Average cost*, exclusive of the fowl, 1*s*. 3*d*. *Sufficient* for 1 entrée.

BRAWN, to make.

Ingredients.—To a pig's head weighing 6 lbs. allow 1½ lb. lean beef, 2 tablespoonfuls of salt, 2 teaspoonfuls of pepper, a little cayenne, 6 pounded cloves. *Mode.*—Cut off the cheeks and salt them, unless the head be small, when all may be used. After carefully cleaning the head, put it on in sufficient cold water to cover it, with the beef, and skim it just before it boils. A head weighing 6 lbs. will require boiling from 2 to 3 hours. When sufficiently boiled to come off the bones easily, put it into a hot pan, remove the bones, and chop the meat with a sharp knife before the fire, together with the beef. *It is necessary to do this as quickly as possible to prevent the fat settling in it.* Sprinkle in the seasoning, which should have been previously mixed. Stir it well and put it quickly into a brawn-tin if you have one; if not, a cake-tin or mould will answer the purpose, if the meat is well pressed with weights, which must not be removed for several hours. When quite cold, dip the tin into boiling water for a minute or two, and the preparation will turn out and be fit for use. *Time.*—From 2 to 3 hours. *Average cost*, for a pig's head, 4½*d*. per lb. *Seasonable* from September to March.

Note.—The liquor in which the head was boiled will make good pea soup, and the fat, if skimmed off and boiled in water, and afterwards poured into cold water, answers the purpose of lard.

BREAD-MAKING.

Panification, or bread-making, consists of the following processes, in the case of Wheaten Flour. Fifty or sixty per cent. of water is added to the flour, with the addition of some leavening matter, and preferably, of yeast from malt and hops. All kinds of leavening matter have, however, been, and are still used in different parts of the world: in the East Indies, "toddy," which is a liquor that flows from the wounded cocoa-nut tree; and in the West Indies, "dunder," or the refuse of the distillation of rum. The dough then undergoes the well-known process called *kneading*. The yeast produces fermentation, a process which may be thus described:—The dough reacting upon the leavening matter introduced, the starch of the flour is transformed into saccharine matter, the saccharine matter being afterwards changed into alcohol and carbonic acid. The dough must be well "bound," and yet allow the escape of the little bubbles of carbonic acid which accompany the fermentation, and which, in their passage, cause the numerous little holes which are seen in light bread.

The yeast must be good and fresh, if the bread is to be digestible and nice. Stale yeast produces, instead of vinous fermentation, an acetous fermentation, which flavours the bread and makes it disagreeable. A poor thin yeast produces an imperfect fermentation, the result being a heavy, unwholesome loaf.

When the dough is well kneaded, it is left to stand for some time, and then, as soon as it begins to swell, it is divided into loaves; after which it is again left to stand, when it once more swells up, and manifests for the last time the symptoms of fermentation. It is then put into the oven, where the water contained in the dough is partly evaporated, and the loaves swell up again, while a yellow crust begins to form upon the surface. When the bread is sufficiently baked, the bottom crust is hard and resonant if struck with the finger, while the crumb is elastic, and rises again after being pressed down with the finger. The bread is, in all probability, baked sufficiently if, on opening the door of the oven, you are met by a cloud of steam, which quickly passes away.

One word as to the unwholesomeness of new bread and hot rolls. When bread is taken out of the oven, it is full of moisture; the starch is held together in masses, and the bread, instead of being crusted so as to expose each grain of starch to the saliva, actually prevents their digestion by being formed by the teeth into leathery poreless masses, which lie on the stomach like so many bullets. Bread should always be at least a day old before it is eaten; and, if properly made, and kept in a *cool dry* place, ought to be perfectly soft and palatable at the end of three or four days. Hot rolls, swimming in melted butter, and new bread, ought to be carefully shunned by everybody who has the slightest respect for that much-injured individual —the Stomach.

AËRATED BREAD.—It is not unknown to some of our readers that Dr. Dauglish, of Malvern, has recently patented a process for making bread "light," without the use of leaven. The ordinary process of bread-making by fermentation is tedious, and much labour of human hands is requisite in the kneading, in order that the dough may be thoroughly interpenetrated with the leaven. The new process impregnates the bread, by the application of machinery, with carbonic acid gas, or fixed air. Different opinions are expressed about the bread; but it is curious to note, that, as corn is now reaped by machinery, and dough is baked by machinery, the whole process of bread-making is probably in course of undergoing changes which will emancipate both the housewife and the professional baker from a large amount of labour.

In the production of Aërated Bread, wheaten flour, water, salt, and carbonic acid gas (generated by proper machinery), are the only materials employed. We need not inform our readers that carbonic acid gas is the source of the effervescence, whether in common water coming from a depth, or in lemonade, or any aërated drink. Its action, in the new bread, takes the place of fermentation in the old.

In the patent process, the dough is mixed in a great iron ball, inside which is a system of paddles, perpetually turning, and doing the kneading part of the business. Into this globe the flour is dropped till it is full, and then the common atmospheric air is pumped out, and the pure gas turned on. The gas is followed by the water, which has been aërated for the purpose, and then begins the churning or kneading part of the business.

Of course, it is not long before we have the dough, and very "light" and nice it looks. This is caught in tins, and passed on to the floor of the oven, which is an endless floor, moving slowly through the fire. Done to a turn, the loaves emerge at the other end of the apartment,—and the Aërated Bread is made.

It may be added, that it is a good plan to change one's baker from time to time, and so secure a change in the quality of the bread that is eaten.

MIXED BREADS.—Rye bread is hard of digestion, and requires longer and slower baking than wheaten bread. It is better when made with leaven of wheaten flour rather than yeast, and turns out lighter. It should not be eaten till two days old. It will keep a long time.

A good bread may be made by mixing rye-flour, wheat-flour, and rice-paste, in equal proportions; also by mixing rye, wheat, and barley. In Norway, it is said that they only bake their barley bread once a year, such is its "keeping" quality.

Indian-corn flour mixed with wheat-flour (half with half) makes a nice bread, but it is not considered very digestible, though it keeps well.

Rice cannot be made into bread, nor can potatoes; but one-third potato-flour to three-fourths wheaten flour makes a tolerably good loaf.

A very good bread, better than the ordinary sort, and of a delicious flavour, is said to be produced by adopting the following recipe:—Take ten parts of wheat-flour, five parts of potato-flour, one part of rice-paste; knead together, add the yeast, and bake as usual. This is, of course, cheaper than wheaten bread.

Flour, when freshly ground, is too glutinous to make good bread, and should therefore not be used immediately, but should be kept dry for a few weeks, and stirred occasionally until it becomes dry, and crumbles easily between the fingers.

Flour should be perfectly dry before being used for bread or cakes; if at all damp, the preparation is sure to be heavy. Before mixing it with the other ingredients, it is a good plan to place it for an hour or two before the fire, until it feels warm and dry.

Yeast from home-brewed beer is generally preferred to any other: it is very bitter, and on that account should be well washed, and put away until the thick mass settles. If it still continues bitter, the process should be repeated; and, before being used, all the water floating at the top must be poured off. German yeast is now very much used, and should be moistened, and thoroughly mixed with the milk or water with which the bread is to be made.

The following observations are extracted from a valuable work on Bread-making, and will be found very useful to our readers:—

The first thing required for making wholesome bread is the utmost cleanliness; the next is the soundness and sweetness of all the ingredients used for it; and, in addition to these, there must be attention and care through the whole process.

An almost certain way of spoiling dough is to leave it half-made, and to allow it to become cold before it is finished. The other most common causes of failure are using yeast which is no longer sweet, or which has been frozen, or has had hot liquid poured over it.

Too small a proportion of yeast, or insufficient time allowed for the dough to rise, will cause the bread to be heavy.

Heavy bread will also most likely be the result of making the dough very hard, and letting it become quite cold, particularly in winter.

COTTAGE LOAF.

If either the sponge or the dough be permitted to overwork itself, that is to say, if the mixing and kneading be neglected when it has reached the proper point for either, sour bread will probably be the consequence in warm weather, and bad bread in any. The goodness will also be endangered by placing it so near the fire as to make any part of it hot, instead of maintaining the gentle and equal degree of heat required for its due fermentation.

Milk or Butter.—Milk which is not perfectly sweet will not only injure the flavour of the bread, but, in sultry weather, will often cause it to be quite uneatable; yet either of them, if *fresh and good*, will materially improve its quality.

To keep bread sweet and fresh, as soon as it is cold it should be put into a clean earthen pan, with a cover to it: this pan should be placed at a little distance from the ground, to allow a current of air to pass underneath. Some persons prefer keeping bread on clean wooden shelves without being covered, that the crust may not soften. Stale bread may be freshened by warming it through in a gentle oven. Stale pastry, cakes, &c., may also be improved by this method.

COTTAGE LOAF.

The utensils required for making bread on a moderate scale, are a kneading-trough or pan, sufficiently large that the dough may be kneaded freely without throwing the flour over the edges, and also to allow for its rising; a hair sieve for straining yeast, and one or two strong spoons.

Yeast must always be good of its kind, and in a fitting state to produce ready and proper fermentation. Yeast of strong beer or ale produces more effect than that of milder kinds; and the fresher the yeast, the smaller the quantity will be required to raise the dough.

As a general rule, the oven for baking bread should be rather quick, and the heat so regulated as to penetrate the dough without hardening the outside. The oven door should not be opened after the bread is put in until the dough is set, or has become firm, as the cool air admitted, will have an unfavourable effect on it.

Brick ovens are generally considered the best adapted for baking bread: these should be heated with wood faggots, and then swept and mopped out, to cleanse them for the reception of the bread. Iron ovens are more difficult to manage, being apt to burn the surface of the bread before the middle is baked. To remedy this, a few clean bricks should be set at the bottom of the oven, close together, to receive the tins of bread. In many modern stoves the ovens are so much improved that they bake admirably; and they can always be brought to the required temperature, when it is higher than is needed, by leaving the door open for a time.

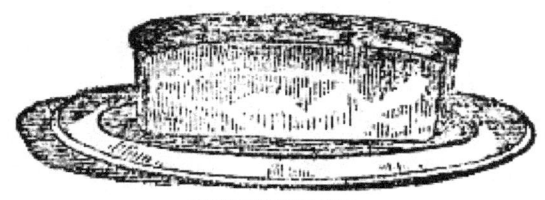

TIN BREAD.

BREAD, to make good Home-made (Miss Acton's Recipe).

Ingredients.—1 quartern of flour, 1 large tablespoonful of solid brewer's yeast, or nearly 1 oz. of fresh German yeast, 1¼ to 1½ pint of warm milk-and-water. *Mode.*—Put the flour into a large earthenware bowl or deep pan; then, with a strong metal or wooden spoon, hollow out the middle; but do not clear it entirely away from the bottom of the pan, as, in that case, the sponge, or leaven (as it was formerly termed) would stick to it, which it ought not to do. Next take either a large tablespoonful of brewer's yeast which has been rendered solid by mixing it with plenty of cold water, and letting it afterwards stand to settle for a day and night; or nearly an ounce of German yeast; put it into a large basin, and proceed to mix it, so that it shall be as smooth as cream, with ¾ pint of warm milk-and-water, or with water only; though even a very little milk will much improve the bread. Pour the yeast into the hole made in the flour, and stir into it as much of that which lies round it as will make a thick batter, in which there must be no lumps. Strew plenty of flour on the top, throw a thick clean cloth over, and set it where the air is warm; but do not place it upon the kitchen fender, for it will become too much heated there. Look at it from time to time: when it has been laid for nearly an hour, and when the yeast has risen and broken through the flour, so that bubbles appear in it, you will know that it is ready to be made up into dough. Then place the pan on a strong chair, or dresser, or table, of convenient height; pour into the sponge the remainder of the warm milk-and-water; stir into it as much of the flour as you can with the spoon; then wipe it out clean with your fingers, and lay it aside. Next take plenty of the remaining flour, throw it on the top of the leaven, and begin, with the knuckles of both hands, to knead it well. When the flour is nearly all kneaded in, begin to draw the edges of the dough towards the middle, in order to mix the whole thoroughly; and when it is free from flour and lumps and crumbs, and does not stick to the hands when touched, it will be done, and may be covered with the cloth, and left to rise a second time. In ¾ hour look at it, and should it have swollen very much and begin to crack, it will be light enough to bake. Turn it then on to a paste-board or very clean dresser, and with a large sharp knife divide it in two; make it up quickly into loaves, and despatch it to the oven: make one or two incisions across the tops of the loaves, as they will rise more easily if this be done. If baked in tins or pans, rub them with a tiny piece of butter laid on a piece of clean paper, to prevent the dough from sticking to them. All bread should be turned upside down, or on its side, as soon as it is drawn from the oven: if this be neglected, the under part of the loaves will become wet and blistered from the steam, which cannot then escape from them. *To make the dough without setting a sponge*, merely mix the yeast with the greater part of the warm milk-and-water, and wet up the whole of the flour at once after a little salt has been stirred in, proceeding exactly, in every other respect, as in the directions just given. As the dough will *soften* in the rising, it should be made quite firm at first, or it will be too lithe by the time it is ready for the oven. *Time.*—To be left to rise an hour the first time, ¾ hour the second time; to be baked from 1 to 1¼ hour, or baked in one loaf from 1½ to 2 hours.

BREAD, to make a Peck of good.

Ingredients.—3 lbs. of potatoes, 6 pints of cold water, ½ pint of good yeast, a peck of flour, 2 oz. of salt. *Mode.*—Peel and boil the potatoes; beat them to a cream while warm; then add 1 pint of cold water, strain through a colander, and add to it ½ pint of good yeast, which should have been put in water over-night to take off its bitterness. Stir all well together with a wooden spoon, and pour the mixture into the centre of the flour; mix it to the substance of cream, cover it over closely, and let it remain near the fire for an hour; then add the 5 pints of water, milk-warm, with 2 oz. of salt; pour this in, and mix the whole to a nice light dough. Let it remain for about 2 hours; then make it into 7 loaves, and bake for about 1½ hour in a good oven. When baked, the bread should weigh nearly 20 lbs. *Time.*—About 1½ hour.

BREAD-AND-BUTTER FRITTERS.

Ingredients.—Batter, 8 slices of bread and butter, 3 or 4 tablespoonfuls of jam. *Mode.*—Make a batter, the same as for apple fritters; cut some slices of bread and butter, not very thick; spread half of them with any jam that may be preferred, and cover with the other slices; slightly press them together, and cut them out in square, long, or round pieces. Dip them in the batter, and fry in boiling lard for about 10 minutes; drain them before the fire on a piece of blotting-paper or cloth. Dish them, sprinkle over sifted sugar, and serve. *Time.*—About 10 minutes. *Average cost,* 1*s*. *Sufficient* for 4 or 5 persons. *Seasonable* at any time.

BREAD-AND-BUTTER PUDDING, Baked.

Ingredients.—9 thin slices of bread and butter, 1½ pint of milk, 4 eggs, sugar to taste, ¼ lb. of currants, flavouring of vanilla, grated lemon-peel, or nutmeg. *Mode.*—Cut 9 slices of bread and butter, not very thick, and put them into a pie-dish, with currants between each layer, and on the top. Sweeten and flavour the milk, either by infusing a little lemon-peel in it, or by adding a few drops of essence of vanilla; well whisk the eggs, and stir these to the milk. *Strain* this over the bread and butter, and bake in a moderate oven for 1 hour, or rather longer. This pudding may be very much enriched by adding cream, candied peel, or more eggs than stated above. It should not be turned out, but sent to table in the pie-dish, and is better for being made about two hours before it is baked. *Time.*—1 hour, or rather longer. *Average cost*, 9*d*. *Sufficient* for 6 or 7 persons. *Seasonable* at any time.

BREAD CRUMBS, Fried.

Cut the bread into thin slices, place them in a cool oven over-night, and when thoroughly dry and crisp, roll them down into fine crumbs. Put some lard, or clarified dripping, into a frying-pan; bring it to the boiling-point, throw in the crumbs, and fry them very quickly. Directly they are done, lift them out with a slice, and drain them before the fire from all greasy moisture. When quite crisp, they are ready for use. The fat they are fried in should be clear, and the crumbs should not have the slightest appearance or taste of having been, in the least degree, burnt.

BREAD, Fried, for Borders.

Proceed by frying some slices of bread, cut in any fanciful shape, in boiling lard. When quite crisp, dip one side of the sippet into the beaten white of an egg mixed with a little flour, and place it on the edge of the dish. Continue in this manner till the border is completed, arranging the sippets a pale and a dark one alternately.

BREAD, Fried Sippets of, for Garnishing many Dishes.

Cut the bread into thin slices, and stamp them out in whatever shape you like,—rings, crosses, diamonds, &c. &c. Fry them in the same manner as the bread-crumbs, in clear boiling lard or clarified dripping, and drain them until thoroughly crisp before the fire. When variety is desired, fry some of a pale colour, and others of a darker hue.

BREAKFASTS.

It will not be necessary to give here a long bill of fare of cold joints, &c., which may be placed on the sideboard, and do duty at the breakfast-table. Suffice it to say, that any cold meat the larder may furnish should be nicely garnished and be placed on the buffet. Collared and potted meats or fish, cold game or poultry, veal-and-ham pies, game-and-rump-steak pies, are all suitable dishes for the breakfast-table; as also cold ham, tongue, &c. &c.

The following list of hot dishes may perhaps assist our readers in knowing what to provide for the comfortable meal called breakfast. Broiled fish, such as mackerel, whiting, herrings, dried haddocks, &c.; mutton chops and rump-steaks, broiled sheep's kidneys, kidneys à la maître d'hôtel, sausages, plain rashers of bacon, bacon and poached eggs, ham and poached eggs, omelets, plain boiled eggs, œufs-au-plat, poached eggs on toast, muffins, toast, marmalade, butter, &c. &c.

In the summer, and when they are obtainable, always have a vase of freshly-gathered flowers on the breakfast-table, and, when convenient, a nicely-arranged dish of fruit: when strawberries are in season, these are particularly refreshing; as also grapes, or even currants.

BRILL.

Ingredients.—¼ lb. of salt to each gallon of water; a little vinegar. *Mode.* —Clean the brill, cut off the fins, and rub it over with a little lemon-juice, to preserve its whiteness. Set the fish in sufficient cold water to cover it; throw in salt, in the above proportions, and a little vinegar, and bring it gradually to boil: simmer very gently, till the fish is done, which will be in about 10 minutes for a small brill, reckoning from the time the water begins to simmer. It is difficult to give the *exact* number of minutes required for cooking a brill, as the fish varies somewhat in thickness, but the cook can always bear in mind that fish of every description should be *very thoroughly dressed*, and never come to table in the *least degree underdone*. The time for boiling of course depends entirely on the size of the fish. Serve it on a hot napkin, and garnish with cut lemon, parsley, horseradish, and a little lobster coral sprinkled over the fish. Send lobster or shrimp sauce and plain melted butter to table with it. *Time.*—After the water boils, a small brill, 10 minutes; a medium sized brill, 15 to 20 minutes; a large brill, ½ hour.

Average cost, from 4*s*. to 8*s*.; but when the market is plentifully supplied, may be had from 2*s*. each. *Seasonable* from August to April.

To choose Brill.—The flesh of this fish, like that of turbot, should be of a yellowish tint, and should be chosen on account of its thickness. If the flesh has a bluish tint, it is not good.

A Brill and John Dory are carved in the same manner as a Turbot.

Note.—The thick parts of the middle of the back are the best slices in a turbot; and the rich gelatinous skin covering the fish, as well as a little of the thick part of the fins, are dainty morsels, and should be placed on each plate.

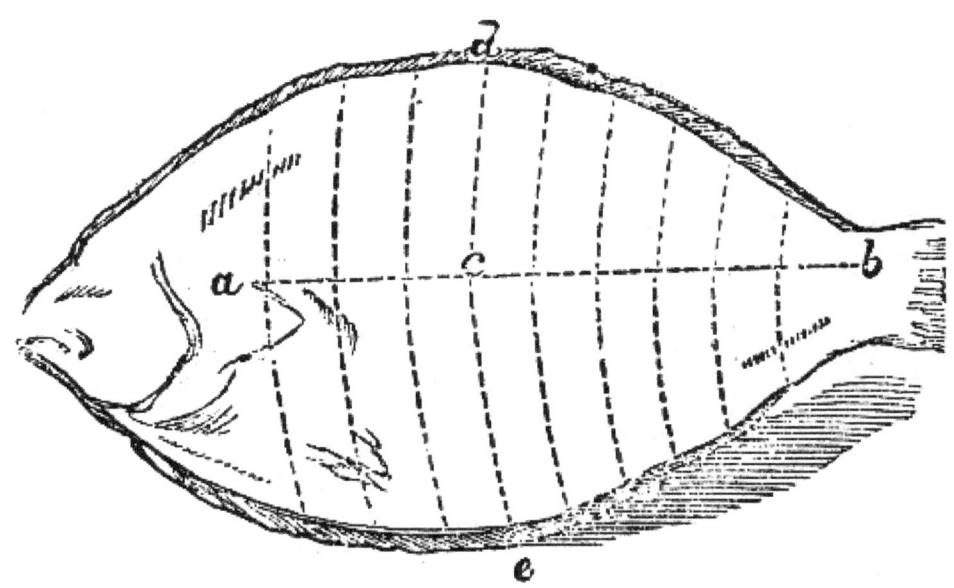

HOW TO CARVE A BRILL.

BROWNING, for Stock.

Ingredients.—2 oz. of powdered sugar, and ½ a pint of water. *Mode.*—Place the sugar in a stewpan over a slow fire until it begins to melt, keeping it stirred with a wooden spoon until it becomes black, when add the water, and let it dissolve. Cork closely, and use a few drops when required.

Note.—In France, burnt onions are made use of for the purpose of browning. As a general rule, the process of browning is to be discouraged, as apt to impart a slightly unpleasant flavour to the stock, and consequently all soups made from it.

BROWNING for Gravies and Sauces.

The browning for stock answers equally well for sauces and gravies, when it is absolutely necessary to colour them in this manner; but where they can be made to look brown by using ketchup, wine, browned flour, tomatoes, or any coloured sauce, it is far preferable. As, however, in cooking so much depends on appearance, perhaps it would be as well for the inexperienced cook to use the artificial means. When no browning is at hand, and you wish to heighten the colour of your gravy, dissolve a lump of sugar in an iron spoon close to a sharp fire; when it is in a liquid state, drop it into the sauce or gravy quite hot. Care, however, must be taken not to put in too much, as it would impart a very disagreeable flavour to the preparation.

BRUSSELS-SPROUTS, Boiled.

Ingredients.—To each ½ gallon of water allow 1 heaped tablespoonful of salt; a *very small* piece of soda. *Mode.*—Clean the sprouts from insects, nicely wash them, and pick off any dead or discoloured leaves from the outsides; put them into a saucepan of *boiling* water, with salt and soda in the above proportion; keep the pan uncovered, and let them boil quickly over a brisk fire until tender; drain, dish, and serve with a tureen of melted butter, or with a maître d'hôtel sauce poured over them. Another mode of serving them is, when they are dished, to stir in about 1½ oz. of butter and a seasoning of pepper and salt. They must, however, be sent to table very quickly, as, being so very small, this vegetable soon cools. Where the cook is very expeditious, this vegetable when cooked may be arranged on the dish in the form of a pineapple, and so served has a very pretty appearance. *Time.*—from 9 to 12 minutes after the water boils. *Average cost*, 1s. 4d. per peck. *Sufficient.*—Allow between 40 and 50 for 5 or 6 persons. *Seasonable* from November to March.

BUBBLE-AND-SQUEAK.

[COLD MEAT COOKERY.] *Ingredients.*—A few thin slices of cold boiled beef; butter, cabbage, 1 sliced onion, pepper and salt to taste. *Mode.*—Fry the slices of beef gently in a little butter, taking care not to dry them up. Lay them on a flat dish, and cover with fried greens. The greens may be prepared from cabbage sprouts or green savoys. They should be boiled till tender, well drained, minced, and placed, till quite hot, in a frying-pan, with butter, a sliced onion, and seasoning of pepper and salt. When the onion is done, it is ready to serve. *Time.*—Altogether, ½ hour. *Average cost*, exclusive of the cold beef, 3*d*. *Seasonable* at any time.

BULLOCK'S HEART, to Dress a.

Ingredients.—1 heart, stuffing of veal forcemeat. *Mode.*—Put the heart into warm water to soak for 2 hours; then wipe it well with a cloth, and, after cutting off the lobes, stuff the inside with a highly-seasoned forcemeat. Fasten it in, by means of a needle and coarse thread; tie the heart up in paper, and set it before a good fire, being very particular to keep it well basted, or it will eat dry, there being very little of its own fat. Two or three minutes before dishing remove the paper, baste well, and serve with good gravy and red-currant jelly or melted butter. If the heart is very large, it will require 2 hours, and, covered with a caul, may be baked as well as roasted. *Time.*—Large heart, 2 hours. *Average cost*, 2*s*. 6*d*. *Sufficient* for 6 or 8 persons. *Seasonable* all the year.

Note.—This is an excellent family dish, is very savoury, and, though not seen at many good tables, may be recommended for its cheapness and economy.

BUNS, Light.

Ingredients.—½ teaspoonful of tartaric acid, ½ teaspoonful of bicarbonate of soda, 1 lb. of flour, 2 oz. of butter, 2 oz. of loaf sugar, ¼ lb. of currants or raisins,—when liked, a few caraway seeds, ½ pint of cold new milk, 1 egg. *Mode.*—Rub the tartaric acid, soda, and flour all together through a hair sieve; work the butter into the flour; add the sugar, currants, and caraway seeds, when the flavour of the latter is liked. Mix all these ingredients well together; make a hole in the middle of the flour, and pour in the milk, mixed with the egg, which should be well beaten; mix quickly, and set the dough, with a fork, on baking-tins, and bake the buns for about 20 minutes. This mixture makes a very good cake, and if put into a tin, should be baked 1½ hour. The same quantity of flour, soda, and tartaric acid, with ½ pint of milk and a little salt, will make either bread or tea-cakes, if wanted quickly. *Time.*—20 minutes for the buns; if made into a cake, 1½ hour. *Sufficient* to make about 12 buns.

BUNS.

BUNS, Plain.

Ingredients.—1 lb. of flour, 6 oz. of good butter, ¼ lb. of sugar, 1 egg, nearly ¼ pint of milk, 2 small teaspoonfuls of baking-powder, a few drops of essence of lemon. *Mode.*—Warm the butter, without oiling it; beat it with a wooden spoon; stir the flour in gradually with the sugar, and mix these ingredients well together. Make the milk lukewarm, beat up with it the yolk of the egg and the essence of lemon, and stir these to the flour, &c. Add the baking-powder, beat the dough well for about 10 minutes, divide it into 24 pieces, put them into buttered tins or cups, and bake in a brisk oven from 20 to 30 minutes. *Time.*—20 to 30 minutes. *Average cost*, 1s. *Sufficient* to make 12 buns. *Seasonable* at any time.

BUNS, Victoria.

Ingredients.—2 oz. of pounded loaf sugar, 1 egg, 1½ oz. of ground rice, 2 oz. of butter, 1½ oz. of currants, a few thin slices of candied-peel, flour. *Mode.*—Whisk the egg, stir in the sugar, and beat these ingredients both together; beat the butter to a cream, stir in the ground rice, currants, and candied-peel, and as much flour as will make it of such a consistency that it may be rolled into 7 or 8 balls. Place these on a buttered tin, and bake them for ½ to ¾ hour. They should be put into the oven immediately or they will become heavy, and the oven should be tolerably brisk. *Time.*—½ to ¾ hour. *Average cost*, 6d. *Sufficient* to make 7 or 8 buns. *Seasonable* at any time.

BUTTER, Browned.

Ingredients.—¼ lb. of butter, 1 tablespoonful of minced parsley, 3 tablespoonfuls of vinegar, salt and pepper to taste. *Mode.*—Put the butter into a frying pan over a nice clear fire, and when it smokes, throw in the parsley, and add the vinegar and seasoning. Let the whole simmer for a minute or two, when it is ready to serve. This is a very good sauce for skate. *Time.*—¼ hour.

BUTTER, Clarified.

Put the butter in a basin before the fire, and when it melts, stir it round once or twice, and let it settle. Do not strain it unless absolutely necessary, as it causes so much waste. Pour it gently off into a clean dry jar, carefully leaving all sediment behind. Let it cool, and carefully exclude the air by means of a bladder, or piece of wash-leather, tied over. If the butter is salt, it may be washed before melting, when it is to be used for sweet dishes.

BUTTER, Curled.

Tie a strong cloth by two of the corners to an iron hook in the wall; make a knot with the other two ends, so that a stick might pass through. Put the butter into the cloth; twist it tightly over a dish, into which the butter will fall through the knot, so forming small and pretty little strings. The butter may then be garnished with parsley, if to serve with a cheese course; or it may be sent to table plain for breakfast, in an ornamental dish. Squirted butter for garnishing hams, salads, eggs, &c., is made by forming a piece of stiff paper in the shape of a cornet, and squeezing the butter in fine strings from the hole at the bottom. Scooped butter is made by dipping a teaspoon or scooper in warm water, and then scooping the butter quickly and thin. In warm weather, it would not be necessary to heat the spoon.

BUTTER, Fairy.

Ingredients.—The yolks of 2 hard-boiled eggs, 1 tablespoonful of orange-flower water, 2 tablespoonfuls of pounded sugar, ¼ lb. of good fresh butter. *Mode.*—Beat the yolks of the eggs smoothly in a mortar, with the orange-flower water and the sugar, until the whole is reduced to a fine paste; add the butter, and force all through an old but clean cloth by wringing the cloth and squeezing the butter very hard. The butter will then drop on the plate in large and small pieces, according to the holes in the cloth. Plain butter may be done in the same manner, and is very quickly prepared, besides having a very good effect.

BUTTER, to keep Fresh.

Butter may be kept fresh for ten or twelve days by a very simple process. Knead it well in cold water till the buttermilk is extracted; then put it in a glazed jar, which invert in another, putting into the latter a sufficient quantity of water to exclude the air. Renew the water every day.

BUTTER, Maître d'Hôtel, for putting into Broiled Fish just before it is sent to Table.

Ingredients.—¼ lb. of butter, 2 dessertspoonfuls of minced parsley, salt and pepper to taste, the juice of 1 large lemon. *Mode.*—Work the above ingredients well together, and let them be thoroughly mixed with a wooden spoon. If this is used as a sauce, it may be poured either under or over the meat or fish it is intended to be served with. *Average cost,* for this quantity, 5*d.*

Note.—4 tablespoonfuls of Béchamel, 2 do. of white stock, with 2 oz. of the above maître d'hôtel butter stirred into it, and just allowed to simmer for 1 minute, will be found an excellent hot maître d'hôtel sauce.

BUTTER, Melted.

Ingredients.—¼ lb. of butter, a dessertspoonful of flour, 1 wineglassful of water, salt to taste. *Mode.*—Cut the butter up into small pieces, put it into a saucepan, dredge over the flour, and add the water and a seasoning of salt; stir it *one way* constantly till the whole of the ingredients are melted and thoroughly blended. Let it just boil, when it is ready to serve. If the butter is to be melted with cream, use the same quantity as of water, but omit the flour; keep stirring it, but do not allow it to boil. *Time.*—1 minute to simmer. *Average cost* for this quantity, 4*d.*

BUTTER, Melted (more Economical).

Ingredients.—2 oz. of butter, 1 dessertspoonful of flour, salt to taste, ½ pint of water. *Mode.*—Mix the flour and water to a smooth batter, which put into a saucepan. Add the butter and a seasoning of salt, keep stirring *one way* till all the ingredients are melted and perfectly smooth; let the whole boil for a minute or two, and serve. *Time.*—2 minutes to simmer. *Average cost* for this quantity, 2*d*.

BUTTER, Rancid, What to do with.

When butter has become very rancid, it should be melted several times by a moderate heat, with or without the addition of water, and as soon as it has been well kneaded, after the cooling, in order to extract any water it may have retained, it should be put into brown freestone pots, sheltered from the contact of the air. The French often add to it, after it has been melted, a piece of toasted bread, which helps to destroy the tendency of the butter to rancidity.

BUTTER, Melted (the French Sauce Blanche).

Ingredients.—¼ lb. of fresh butter, 1 tablespoonful of flour, salt to taste, ½ gill of water, ½ spoonful of white vinegar, a very little grated nutmeg. *Mode.*—Mix the flour and water to a smooth batter, carefully rubbing down with the back of a spoon any lumps that may appear. Put it in a saucepan with all the other ingredients, and let it thicken on the fire, but do not allow it to boil, lest it should taste of the flour. *Time.*—1 minute to simmer. *Average cost*, 5*d*. for this quantity.

BUTTER, Melted, made with Milk.

Ingredients.—1 teaspoonful of flour, 2 oz. of butter, ½ pint of milk, a few grains of salt. *Mode.*—Mix the butter and flour smoothly together on a plate, put it into a lined saucepan, and pour in the milk. Keep stirring it *one way* over a sharp fire; let it boil quickly for a minute or two, and it is ready to serve. This is a very good foundation for onion, lobster, or oyster sauce: using milk instead of water makes it look much whiter and more delicate. *Time.*—Altogether, 10 minutes. *Average cost* for this quantity, 3*d*.